India B

Dekho Apna Bharat

VARUN SONI

ZORBA BOOKS

ZORBA BOOKS

Published by Zorba Books, July 2024
Website: www.zorbabooks.com
Email: info@zorbabooks.com
Author Name: Varun Soni
Copyright ©: Varun Soni

Title: India Beyond Metros

Printbook ISBN: 978-93-5896-618-3
Ebook ISBN: 978-93-5896-120-1

All rights reserved. No part of this book may be reproduced or transmitted in any form or by any means, electronic or mechanical, except by a reviewer. The reviewer may quote brief passages, with attribution, in a review to be printed in a magazine, newspaper, or on the Web—without permission in writing from the copyright owner.

The publisher under the guidance and direction of the author has published the contents in this book, and the publisher takes no responsibility for the contents, its accuracy, completeness, any inconsistencies, or the statements made. The contents of the book do not reflect the opinion of the publisher or the editor. The publisher and editor shall not be liable for any errors, omissions, or the reliability of the contents of the book.

Any perceived slight against any person/s, place or organization is purely unintentional.

Zorba Books Pvt. Ltd. (opc)
Sushant Arcade,
Next to Courtyard Marriot,
Sushant Lok 1, Gurgaon – 122009, India

Printed by Manipal Technologies Limited
A1 & A2 Shivalli Industrial Area Manipal Udupi, Karnataka – 57610

Dedicated to my parents, Kamini Soni and Dr Purshotam Lal Soni, who have always supported me in whatever I do… unconditionally.

Contents

Introduction .... *vii*

Jabalpur 1
Vijaywada 5
Hubballi 8
Kollam 11
Thanjavur 14
Kolhapur 17
Jamnagar 20
Gorakhpur 23
Jodhpur 26
Amritsar 30
Jammu 33
Gwalior 36
Bhubaneswar 39
Nellore 42
Belagavi 45
Thrissur 48
Vadodara and Bharuch 51
Kota 54
Prayagraj 57
Deoghar 60
Guwahati 63

Contents

Coimbatore	66
Udaipur	69
Ujjain	73
Darbhanga	76
Mangaluru	79
Surat	82
Bikaner	85
Raipur	89
Rajamahendravaram	92
Tiruchirappalli	95
Kozhikode	98
Chhatrapati Sambhaji Nagar	101
Kanpur	106
Visakhapatnam	109
Mysuru	113
Siliguri	117
Rajkot and Junagadh	120
Indore	124
Varanasi	128
Kannur	132
Madurai	136
Bhuj	139
Udupi	143
Warangal	147
Chandigarh	150
Puri	154
Ranchi	158
Nashik and Shirdi	161
Shivamogga	165

Introduction

Since 2010, thanks to my various professional assignments, I have been travelling across the length and breadth of India to Tier 2 and 3 cities and in most cases, passing through Bharat's hinterland. What I noticed was that there is so much to see in our own country which many are not even aware of.

For instance, I was not aware of the beauty of North Kerala or Coastal Karnataka; the majesty of the Brihadesvara Temple at Thanjavur; the Kanaka Durga Temple in Vijaywada or the Mahalaxmi Temple in Kolhapur; the historical significance of Jamnagar; the innumerable waterfalls cascading down the mountains in cities located in the Western Ghats; the beauty and peace of the Krishna-Godavari Sangam, et al.

Generally, most urban middle class across metropolitan areas frequent places like Agra, Jaipur, Udaipur, Himachal, Uttarakhand, Ooty, Darjeeling, Munnar and the backwaters of Kerala for vacations. Have you ever heard of anyone visiting Jabalpur, Gorakhpur, Hubballi, Shivamogga, Kollam, Rajahmahendravaram, etc?

This is the vacuum that *'India Beyond Metros: Dekho Apna Bharat,'* fills in.

The book contains 50-odd chapters, each chapter dedicated to one city spelling out what to see, where to stay, how to go, and even what to shop for. *'India Beyond Metros: Dekho Apna Bharat'* is ideal for corporate travellers who visit these cities for official work or

Introduction

families who want to spend holidays/ weekends exploring their own country.

In many cities, I have been told that people come from the nearby region to either worship in renowned temples or just spend their holidays amidst nature. In fact, recently on a visit to Shivamogga in Central Karnataka, my cab driver was getting calls from tourists from Chennai who were reaching the next day. On asking what they come here for, the driver answered, "Sir, there are a few temples in the area that lots of people frequent and coupled with the wildlife sanctuaries, people make Shivamogga a focal point to explore Karnataka."

That's when I realised that tourists from nearby cities or regions are the ones driving tourism in these cities. Whilst people in the metros are busy making plans for Thailand, Bali, Maldives, Dubai or Europe.

But it's time to look inward. Inwards into Bharat, that is, India. An ancient civilisation that has weathered many storms and witnessed many seasons. This is evident from the innumerable monuments and temples that are strewn across the length and breadth of the country.

Apart from history, you will also get to read about the exquisite natural beauty of some cities and their surrounding areas. This don't find a mention in leading travel journals.

'India Beyond Metros: Dekho Apna Bharat' makes you aware of the potential of Bharat and the treasure that is hidden in our smaller cities, kasbas, and the hinterland.

Read the book, identify your next vacation bucket list and… Vroom you Go!

Jabalpur

•••

On the Map:

Jabalpur is an important city located in the Mahakaushal region of Madhya Pradesh. It has historical significance, having been the centre of Kalachuri and Gond dynasties. Jabalpur is situated on the banks of the River Narmada.

Flying Down:

Though Jabalpur has a small airport (Dumna, which is 20 km from the city) boasting only one conveyor belt, it is connected to major metros in India like Delhi, Mumbai and Hyderabad. Also connected to Indore, Raipur and Prayagraj and well connected by train and road, to all major urban centres in the country. Recently, Vande Bharat Express started services between Bhopal and Jabalpur.

Moving Around:

I have visited this city thrice and always felt that the best part of Jabalpur is its immense green cover, which you see as soon as you exit the airport. The road from the airport to the city passes through lush greenery and a very big cantonment area that has been beautifully designed and maintained.

The cantonment gives way to palatial bungalows, and if you are a first-time visitor, that might impress you and make you wonder about the growing local economy of the region. The cantonment is also lined with very trendy cafes and shopping outlets.

Once you are in the city, it might feel a trifle overgrown, but with a number of ongoing infrastructure projects in the city, the look and feel is expected to improve soon.

Jabalpur city itself has nothing much to offer, but if you do go there either on a personal or official trip, your visit would be incomplete without seeing the spectacular Dhuandhar waterfalls at Bhedaghat, a 30-minute drive from the city. Cabs are easily available for the same. The waterfalls are known as the mini-Niagara of India. If you visit in and around monsoon, you are bound to see it in all its splendor with the Narmada waters in full force.

During the monsoon season, the water gushes so fast that its roar is heard from afar, creating a magical mist that is difficult to miss. The first time I visited, I went through the usual tourist route and witnessed the splendor of the waterfalls from up, close, and personal, especially from a point near to the waters. What takes your breath away are the pure white marble rocks onto which the water falls, adding to the uniqueness of the natural wonder.

When you get into Bhedaghat town, try to have lunch at the MP Tourism restaurant atop a hill, giving you spectacular views of the river meandering its way in between gigantic rocks below.

On my second visit and thanks to my friend, Koushalendra Mahajan, I witnessed the splendor of the Dhuandhar falls from the other side, through the lawns of another MP Tourism property aptly called Marble Rocks. It gives beautiful views of the rocks opposite and of the river making its way below. I even saw a man jumping thousands of feet from the rocks into the river periodically, on-demand from tourists.

You can take your cab beyond the resort and see the marble rocks canyon from different vantage points along the path.

Note of Caution: Be careful not to go close to the edge to click selfies as one slip can cost you your life.

There is also a ropeway near the Marble Rocks resort that enables the tourists to see the canyon in all its splendor and also the Narmada from the air at Rs 150 per person.

Near the waterfalls is also the famous and ancient 11th-century Chausath Yogini Temple which has 81 shrines instead of 64 as the name suggests. It is 5 km from Jabalpur and is a famous pilgrim centre. It is one of the few remaining Yogini temples in the country that is dedicated to various Hindu goddesses.

On the way back from Dhuandhar, stop at the Bargi dam. You can take a walk on the terrace of the dam, which on one side looks down upon the river gushing out from the dam's gates, and on the other overlooks the tranquil reservoir.

Further down the route, on the banks of the reservoir, is an MP Tourism resort that offers rooms, boating trips and a nice restaurant with decent food.

The lush greens flanking the road back to Jabalpur will make you feel satisfied with a trip well spent.

Staying in Comfort:

Jabalpur might not have any branded luxury or business hotels, but it has its own crop of local brands like Hotel Satya Ashok: A Government Hotel which is decent and comfortable and located bang in the city centre; The luxurious and famous Hotel Vijan Mahal resembles a palace and is vastly popular among the local swish set for dinners, parties and get-togethers; There are other hotels too, like Hotel Prince Viraj and Shawn Elizey that are basically built for hosting marriage parties, but offer a comfortable stay. The plus point with them is that during non-marriage season, rooms are easily available here.

What to Buy:

Jabalpur is famous for its chikki with Lucky Chikki Centre being the best go-to place to buy the famous Indian snack.

Vijaywada

•••

On the Map:

Located on the banks of the River Krishna stands the ancient city of Vijaywada, the second largest metropolis in Andhra Pradesh.

Legend goes that this is where Goddess Durga killed the demon Mahishasur, which is why the city is called Vijaywada – Vijay means victory and Wada denoting gate which makes Vijaywada the Gateway to Victory.

Flying Down:

Vijaywada's Gannavaram Airport is an international airport with flights to South-East Asia and the Gulf. Domestically, Vijaywada has direct flights to Hyderabad, Bengaluru, Delhi and Chennai.

Rail and road connectivity are at best as is for any major city.

Moving Around:

When I first landed in Vijaywada, I was struck by the wide roads and well-planned urban infrastructure. The city is organised, is a cultural hub of Andhra Pradesh with a lot of historical and religious significance.

The city centre, Benz Circle and the surrounding MG Road are lined on both sides with commercial complexes and shopping malls. As is the case with most of South India, the city is home to a number of local saree showrooms that span four floors and sell everything from sarees to menswear and kidswear.

While the city itself gives you a welcome vibe, the best place to visit while on a trip to Vijaywada is the Kanaka Durga Temple. Perched atop the Indrakeeladri hills overlooking the Krishna River, the Temple features a resplendent deity in gold, all decked in ornaments. While driving up the meandering road to the temple, you can stop on a bend to catch a glimpse of the city and river below. You get a similar view from the terrace of the temple.

Since the temple complex is huge, be aware of the route as your taxi would be parked at the entrance and if you exit via the normal route, you might end up at the bottom of the hill, as happened with me. The prasadam (*laddoo*) is also available at the exit point.

But, after buying the prasadam, I realised that I could not even contact my driver as mobiles are not allowed inside the temple. Hence, I had no choice but to climb over 100 steps back to the top of the hill, barefoot, on stairs full of Kumkum and haldi.

Opposite the temple downhill is the Prakasam Barrage on the Krishna River where you can even drive across the bridge on a road that winds its way along the river. Located here, 10 km from the city, are the Undavalli caves, a fine example of ancient Indian rock-cut temples.

If you want an even closer feel of the river, travel 30 km from the city to Ibrahimpatnam to see the Pavitra Sangam – the confluence of the sacred Krishna-Godavari rivers. Once you turn from the highway and take inside roads to reach the Sangam, you will be pleasantly surprised to see the whole area that has been developed into ghats, gardens, children's play area and boating activities on the river. Every evening, thousands of people throng the Sangam for recreational purposes.

If local art interests you, you can also visit Kondapalli village, some 20-odd km away from Vijaywada, which is home to the famous Kondapalli wooden toys. Available in a riot of colours, they are a must-have souvenir from the city.

Staying in Comfort:

Vijaywada is home to many big brands in the hospitality sector like Vivanta, Lemon Tree, Novotel, Red Fox, WelcomHotel and Hyatt to name a few.

What to Buy:

Vijaywada is famous for the Andhra Pochampalli and Pattu sarees, antiques, pearl jewellery, and the famed Kondapalli toys. Take your Pick!

Hubballi

• • •

On the Map:

Located in North Karnataka, the twin cities of Hubballi-Dharwad are a major education centre in the region and the country. The highway between the two cities is strewn with regional and private engineering and medical colleges. Together they constitute the second largest city in Karnataka after Bengaluru.

Flying Down:

Earlier, Hubballi was only connected to Bengaluru through ATR aircraft, but now the city is connected directly to Mumbai, Chennai, Hyderabad and Delhi as well. It is a mere 8 km from the main city.

Moving Around:

While the Old City, as in most cities across India, is as congested as it can be, the newer areas are more spread out and well-planned. This is also where most of the happening hotels are located.

The city is surrounded by the Western Ghats, arguably the most green and beautiful part of India, providing it with a hilly shield. The most popular place to visit on your trip to Hubballi is the Sidharoodha Math, built in remembrance of the celebrated Shri Sidharoodha Swamy.

A big gate built in Kannada-style architecture welcomes you 800 metres away from the Math. The Math itself is a big complex with two big halls where scores of people sits meditating in peace or paying obeisance to the Saint. It has been designed keeping in mind the aesthetics of a Hindu pilgrim site. Since thousands of devotees throng it on a daily basis, it has become a tourist destination in itself and is thus flanked on all sides with eateries and puja shopping outlets.

Hubballi is blessed to have a big water body called the Unkal Lake that enables the evenings in the city to remain cool after the scorching heat of the afternoon. You will see local residents flocking to its shore after sunset and a number of street food vendors lining its boulevard offering sumptuous Indian snacks. The lake also offers recreational opportunities like boating and water sports.

Near the Unkal lake is situated the exquisite Chandramouleshwara Temple. Dedicated to Lord Shiva, the 900-year-old temple is built in the Chalukyan style of architecture and the large courtyard with its four gates and the ancient place of worship will surely transport you into the annals of spirituality.

Staying in Comfort:

While Hubballi does have branded properties like Lemon Tree, Fortune, the Fern, it is the local brands that take the cake. The Naveen Lakeside is bang on the Unkal Lake and the view from the rooms and the hotel is breathtaking.

The President is opposite the lake with an equally appealing view, giving you the opportunity to take a stroll in the evening.

What to Buy:

Any trip is incomplete without buying a pack of the famed Dharwad Peda from Hubballi-Dharwad. The famous sweet shop has outlets and can be seen at every major nook and corner of the twin cities. It now has a rival named Mishra Peda.

Kollam

• • •

On the Map:

Known as Quilon during the British rule, the port city of Kollam in South Kerala is situated 71 km from Thiruvananthapuram (a 2-hour drive), on the banks of the beautiful Ashtamudi backwaters. Ashtamudi is considered the gateway to the backwaters in Kerala and the Ashtamudi to Alapuzzha route on a houseboat is famous for its scenic journey.

Flying Down:

There is no airport in Kollam, so the best way to get there is to go via Thiruvananthapuram. For those preferring the rail route, the Thiruvananthapuram-Kasaragod Vande Bharat Express has a stop at Kollam junction.

Moving Around:

Kollam is a must if you are visiting Thiruvananthapuram or on a tour of Kerala. Generally, tour operators do not include the city in their Kerala itinerary and only the discerning traveller knows what the city has to offer.

The biggest attraction in Kollam is the Ashtamudi Lake and luckily my hotel was bang on its shore, with the room overlooking the backwaters. My hotel (Hotel All Season) even offered a one-hour houseboat cruise on the backwaters. Being a rivulet, the lake is calm and serene, lined with lush greenery on all sides, giving way to Kerala style courtyard homes in between.

Apart from the Ashtamudi lake, Kollam also has a long beach called the Mahatma Gandhi Beach with a clear set sandy stretch albeit with high waves. In the evening the beach and its broadwalk are full of people taking a jog, chit-chatting, couples and youngsters having ice cream or coconut water, etc.

However, a MUST VISIT when in Kollam is Jatayu Park, which is located one hour away from the city in the midst of the Western Ghats. The sculpture of Jatayu is so spectacular that you are bound to get mesmerised upon visiting it.

Your journey starts when you take a left from the Thiruvananthapuram highway and drive along the road leading to the Jatayu Adventure Centre from the highway winding its way through lush green countryside lined with small villages.

Once you reach the Centre, you need to buy tickets for a trolley that takes you uphill to the Jatayu Park. The journey up gives you a glimpse of the beauty of the Western Ghats, but as soon as you alight from the trolley and venture out into the open, you are simply awestruck.

The world's largest bird sculpture of the slain Jatayu (as per Ramayana) has been made so painstakingly by architect Rajiv Anchal that it literally transports you into the world of mythology. You can take a tour around the sculpture going in between its big feather. A Jatayu Earth Centre inside the sculpture houses a 6D theatre narrating the legend of Jatayu.

The Centre also has a Rama Temple, an amphitheatre and many adventure sports activities to give a complete, wholesome experience.

Staying in Comfort:

Apart from other city hotels, there are two hotels located on the banks of the Ashtamudi Lake – All Season and Raviz. Their location is brilliant and with rooms overlooking the backwaters is a definite must-stay from my side.

What to Buy:

Kollam is famous for its Pattu sarees and cashewnuts. Most people in India are unaware that Kollam is the Cashew Capital of the World, being the largest exporter of processed cashew. Hence, buying cashew nuts is a given when visiting Kollam.

Thanjavur

•●•

On the Map:
Previously known as Tanjore, Thanjavur was the seat of the great Chola empire and is located near the east coast of Tamil Nadu, in the delta region of the Cauvery River. Having great cultural and religious significance, Thanjavur is the place where most of the amazing Chola temples are located. Apart from this, it is a big silk weaving centre and home to the famous Tanjore paintings.

Flying Down:

The nearest airport to Thanjavur is Tiruchirappalli, which is connected to Chennai, Bengaluru and Hyderabad. Tiruchirappalli is 66 km, a one-hour drive from Thanjavur. Thanjavur is well connected via road and rail to major urban centres like Chennai, Madurai, Tiruchirappalli and Puducherry.

Moving Around:

Thanjavur is synonymous with the magnificent Brihadeeswara Temple built more than 1000 years ago on the banks of the River Cauvery. No trip to Thanjavur is complete without seeing the resplendent Brihadeeswara Temple. Built in true Chola style of architecture, the Shaivaite Temple is the mainstay of the city and can be seen from afar. I would suggest visiting it in the evening around 5 pm so that one can witness its full glory as the lights come on, once the sun sets.

The entire temple complex is made from rocks, with the kumbam (the top of the structure with 80 tons) and the Giant Nandi, both carved out of a single rock respectively. The Temple complex has two huge gates replete with carved figures of Hindu Gods and Goddesses in true South Indian style of temple architecture.

As you enter the complex through the second gate, you can see a huge courtyard with two big temples. From them the smaller one is for Goddess Parvati and the bigger one is for Lord Shiva. Outside the Temple of Goddess Parvati, stands the giant Nandi in black granite. The whole complex is a mix of well-manicured lawns, small temples and carved figures.

Other places to visit in Thanjavur include the Vijaynagar Fort, the Maratha Palace with the museum within and the street outside the palace that is lined with Tanjore painting shops.

Stay in Comfort:

Thanjavur has many options in the CAT 3 category of hotels. But the best and nearest hotel to the Temple is Hotel Sangam. An old property that has large spacious rooms, the hotel is popular and oldest in its category among tourists. Hotel Parisutham is another good choice.

Thanjavur also has good natural retreats like the Great Trails River View Resort and the Svatma Heritage Hotel that offer comfortable stays for the discerning traveller.

What to Buy:

The most apparent thing you can buy in Thanjavur is the Tanjore painting, made in rich and vivid colours with glittering gold foils. Though one can find them at emporiums all over India, it is best to buy from the city where they originated.

As mentioned earlier, most of the studios of painters are lined outside the Maratha Palace. They are as good as any from a fancy emporium. I bought a painting depicting the Shiva Family from one such painter, and believe me, it's exquisite and creatively painted.

You can also buy the Thanjavur Plates in silver, bronze and copper depicting gods and goddesses. The Thanjavur dancing doll makes for a pretty décor item for your home.

Kolhapur

• • •

On the Map:

Situated on the banks of the Panchganga river in South West Maharashtra, Kolhapur has always been famous for the Mahalaxmi Temple and the Kolhapuri chappal. Also referred to as Dakshin Kashi due to its religious sanctity, Shahu Maharaj was one of the greatest rulers of Kolhapur before the British annexation.

Flying Down:

While rail and road connectivity to and from Kolhapur is good, the city recently witnessed the opening of a small airport where flights are now available for Mumbai, Bengaluru, and Hyderabad.

Travellers from other parts of the country can now hop and fly across to Kolhapur easily.

Moving Around:

As you move out of the small airport of Kolhapur, the mesmerising view of the green carpet that engulfs the area leading up to the city, will rejuvenate you. After check-in to my hotel, I moved around the city and my first stop was the Rankala Lake. A man-made lake built by Chhatrapati Shahu Maharaj, the Rankala Lake has two ghats – the Rajghat and the Marathaghat. The best time to visit here is the evening when the breeze turns cool and you can even partake in street food from the numerous food stalls lining the boulevard.

The most famous place with which the city of Kolhapur is synonymous is the Mahalaxmi Temple. One of the fifty-one Shaktipeeth's in India, the Temple was built during the Chalukya rule and embodies ancient South Indian architecture. What is remarkable in the way it has been constructed is that for 2-3 days in a year, the sun's rays fall on the deity's feet climbing up covering it fully during sunset. This phenomenon is even celebrated as Kirnotsav. If you want to visit during this time which mostly falls in the month of November, please book your hotel in advance.

When I visited Kolhapur, it was the monsoon season and my driver took me to the ghats of the Panchganga river. The river was in full spate and looking ethereal with its waters gushing downwards towards the Arabian Sea. Proper ghats have been made there to give you the opportunity to sit in solace on the banks of the Panchganga.

Another place of tourist attraction in Kolhapur is the New Palace, built in the 19th century, serving as the home of Chhatrapati Shahu Maharaj. Its architecture is a mix of Rajwada, Marathi and

Gujarati styles. You can get a peek into the Royal Family's lifestyle by visiting the museum located on the ground floor.

Other places to see in and around Kolhapur are the Panhala Fort and the Kopeshwar Temple dedicated to Lord Shiva. Nature afficionados/lovers can also take out time to visit the Dajipur and the Sagareshwar Wildlife Sanctuaries.

Stay in Comfort:

I stayed at Sayyaji Hotel in Kolhapur, which is an Indore-based hotel chain that has hotels in Central and Western India. The hotel is simply WOW. Never come across a hotel in a Tier 2 city that has been designed with such grandeur and opulence.

Apart from Sayyaji, there is Hotel Classic Midtown, Regenta Place Raysons for a comfortable stay in the city.

What to Buy:

Obviously, the Kolhapuri Chappal. You can buy the T-strapped sandals in leather in all shapes and sizes at Mahadwar, Shivaji or Bahusinghji road. Women can buy traditional Maharashtrian jewellery like the Kolhapuri Saaj or Thushi.

Jamnagar

On the Map:

More popular for being home to Reliance Industries, Jamnagar is the fifth largest city in Gujarat, located south of the Gulf of Kutch in Saurashtra region of the state. Earlier, it was a princely state, and the city is also where noted cricketers Ranji Singh and Duleep Singh resided, after whom the famous Ranji Trophy and Duleep Trophy are named. Current cricketing sensation Ravindra Jadeja also hails from Jamnagar.

Flying Down:

Jamnagar does not have an airport of its own. The nearest airport is Rajkot, which is less than two hours away. Rajkot is well connected to Delhi, Mumbai, and Bengaluru.

Moving Around:

A city of palaces and temples, Jamnagar has always been a popular city since the medieval ages. Its Maharaja gave shelter to 1,000 Polish children during World War II, when other nations were unwilling to help.

The first and foremost place to visit in Jamnagar is the Ranmal Lake around which the whole city revolves. The lake is a popular hangout with locals and has beautiful walkways and gardens for people to chill, relax and kids to play. There are jharokhas all around the boundary of the lake wherein you can sit and enjoy the serenity of the shimmering waters.

In the middle of the lake is the Lakhota Palace built in the 19th century boasting of architecture that is a mix of Gujarati and British styles. The Palace also houses a museum that showcases artefacts, sculptures, weapons and other lifestyle ornaments associated with the royal family.

Another royal property worth seeing is the Darbarbagh Palace which looks marvellous with its large courtyards, sprawling gardens, ornate interiors, imposing arches and carved out façade.

Other places to see in the city are the Pratap Vilas Palace and the Swaminarayan Temple, known for its intricately carved exterior and mesmerising architecture, representing Gujarati culture.

If you have an extra day on your hands, try to visit the Narara Marine National Park, which is more than an hour's drive from Jamnagar. The National Park is home to coral reefs which you can see up, close and personal without having to dive into the waters. You can just walk in the water which will be 1-2 feet up your legs and witness the fascinating world of sea life including corals, fish, octopus and crabs.

Just half-an-hour away from the city is the Khijadiya Bird Sanctuary, a paradise for nature lovers and bird watchers. Spread over 600 hectares of marshes and mangroves, Khijadiya is home to more than 200 species of migratory birds.

You can even club a visit to the revered Dwarkadhish Temple in Dwarka, 2.5 hours away from Jamnagar. One of the Char Dhams in India, the Temple is believed to be Lord Krishna's Capital where he lived with his wife Rukmini.

Stay in Comfort:

Indore based Sayyaji Group's hotel in Jamnagar by the same name, is probably one of the best hotels in the city. Other top hotels are Hotel Aram, Lords Eco Inn and Anaya Beacon.

What to Buy:

Like most of Gujarat, you can buy tie and dye Bandhini fabrics, sarees or suit material from Jamnagar apart from gold embroidery and metalware. Mahavir Bandhni and Chandni Bazaar are some go to places for shopping.

Gorakhpur

•●•

On the Map:

Situated in Eastern Uttar Pradesh, Gorakhpur derives its name from the renowned saint, Gorakhnath, who was an ascetic and a prominent member of the Nath Sampradaya. Located along the Rapti River, the city is near the Nepal border and has always been the gateway for people travelling to the Himalayan country by road.

Flying Down:

Gorakhpur has flight connectivity with major metros like Delhi, Mumbai, Kolkata and Hyderabad. By road, the link between the city and the Purvanchal Expressway will be operational soon and hence coming from Delhi will be a seamless and comfortable drive.

Moving Around:

I was pleasantly surprised to see the infrastructure at Gorakhpur – wide roads, promenade around the big lake, well managed traffic around tourist places – completely negating my apprehensions about visiting this city. I carried the impression of a congested UP city with pot-holed roads and dilapidated buildings, but I was obviously in for a pleasant shock.

The most prominent place to visit when in Gorakhpur is the Gorakhnath Temple. A Temple of the Nath monastic group, the Gorakhnath Temple is named after an ascetic by the same name. His tomb too is located inside the complex, which houses temples of all Gods and Goddesses. A cultural hub of the city, the Temple even has a guest house and a meditation hall within its beautifully designed compound.

The other main attraction of the city is the Gita Press headquarters. (Gita Press is the world's oldest and largest publisher of Hindu religious books.) The main entrance of Gita Press's headquarters in Gorakhpur is a sight to behold. The architecture of the gate incorporates the Ajanta and Ellora caves with the head part being a replica of the Meenakshi Temple in Madurai. A pic with the entrance is must for your insta handle.

Opposite the Gita Press headquarters is their publishing store, where all Hindu religious books are available in different volumes in Hindi and English.

Other places to visit in Gorakhpur are the Railway Museum, the Imambara and the shimmering Ramgarh Taal. The lake is a must go in the evening wherein you can walk along the promenade, go boating or just chill while sitting and looking at the sun setting against its waters.

If you can spare an extra day in Gorakhpur, then I suggest visiting Kushinagar, which is less than 2 hours away (55 km). Kushinagar is a popular tourist destination in the Budhist circuit and is home to the Dying Buddha sculpture. Kushinagar has Buddhist Temples from various countries like Myanmar, China, Sri Lanka, Thailand, and Korea.

More than three hours away on a different route from Gorakhpur and inside Nepalese territory is Kapilvastu, where Lord Buddha spent 29 years of his life and Lumbini, where he was born. Both places have huge religious significance and can be visited on a day trip from Gorakhpur.

Stay in Comfort:

Probably the best place to stay in Gorakhpur is the Marriott Courtyard and the Radisson Blu Hotels. Located on the road to the airport, Radisson hotel is synonymous with luxury and is the most popular in the city. You can see the Ramgarh Taal from the hotel as the lift climbs to the top floors. Newly opened is the Marriott Courtyard in Nauka Vihar directly opposite the lake promenade.

The second best option is Nirvana Sarovar Portico, located on the other side of the lake. It spells comfort from the word go.

What to Buy:

Religious books from Gita Press are the best thing to buy from Gorakhpur. The bookstore offers ayurvedic products as well.

Jodhpur

On the Map:

Famous for the awe inspiring Mehrangarh Fort that towers over the city, Jodhpur is the second largest city in Rajasthan and is located in the North-West part of the state. Historically, the capital of the Marwar region in Rajasthan, Jodhpur is also known as the Blue City of India. It is because most of the houses and buildings built in the medieval era in Old City are hued in shades of blue.

Flying Down:

Jodhpur is well connected by air to all major cities like Delhi, Mumbai, Hyderabad, Bengaluru and Chennai. It also has an excellent road and rail network. For a larger trip to Rajasthan, travellers include it also with Jaisalmer and Bikaner.

Moving Around:

Mehrangarh Fort and the Umaid Bhawan Palace are must-see items on everyone's bucket list when they travel to Jodhpur. Rising above the Blue City, located on a hilltop, the Mehrangarh Fort is every bit the quintessential Rajasthani fortress built during medieval times. It offers a spectacular picture of the city and gives you an instagrammable view of the city, hued in blue below. The Fort includes a museum that houses all the paraphernalia including weapons, costumes, jewellery and furniture associated with the royal family.

Located nearby is the intricately carved, white marble cenotaph of Maharaja Jaswant Singh II called the Jaswant Thada. You can relax in its sprawling lawns, overlooking the Mehrangarh Fort and enjoy the stunning view especially at sunset as the sun's evening rays illuminate the historical masterpiece.

For the adventurous, Mehrangarh Fort also has a zip-line above, to give you an adrenalin rush. Next to the Fort is the Rao Jodha Desert Rock Park which houses rock plant varieties and even has a walking track for those who enjoy trekking.

While winding your way down from the Mehrangarh Fort, you can explore the lanes and bylanes of the Blue City, stopping at each turn to take photographs or selfies against the indigo-coloured walls. Wearing something in contrast to blue will make you stand out.

The bustling (though congested) Old City's best landmark is the Clock Tower around which, in the square as well as its lanes and bylanes, are located shops that sell tie and dye sarees, dupattas, home furnishings, spices, jewellery etc. Many tourist companies organise walking tours in the lanes giving you a glimpse of an era gone by, plus giving you an opportunity to buy local handicrafts.

There are several cafes that have sprung up on the first floors of buildings around the clock tower, letting you relax in their balconies looking down as life goes by.

There is a step-well located near the Clock Tower that is a must see. It has been restored as the steps have been sand plastered and the water regenerated. There is even a café now that overlooks the well, giving you a view of history.

A 10-minute walk from the step-well will bring you to Gulab Sagar. The walled lake with jharokhas all around is a perfect spot to take pictures as the Mehrangarh Fort towers behind on the hilltop.

However, the most exquisite and magnificent masterpiece of Jodhpur is the Umaid Bhawan Palace. One of the last palaces to be built in India, the Umaid Bhawan has been the backdrop for many Hollywood and Indian movies as well as celebrity weddings. It is spectacular, grandiose and luxury par excellence. Part of it serves as the residence of the current Maharaja, while the remaining is now a luxury hotel. Those who are not in-house guests can also visit and take a tour of the hotel's public quarters to see its opulence.

Other places to visit are the Mandore Garden with its exquisite collection of temples, chhatris and rock cut terraces. Near Mandore is the Kaylana Lake that looks resplendent during the day.

On the banks of the Balsamand Lake is the palace hotel of the same name. It makes for a luxurious stay with its sprawling lawns, beautiful hut shaped rooms, a stable for horses and palace rooms overlooking the lake.

Stay in Comfort:

Be it heritage properties or new age luxuries, all big brands have properties in Jodhpur. So much so that the traveller will get spoilt for choice and they come in all shapes and sizes as well as in all price ranges. You have the ultra-luxurious Umaid Bhawan, Ajit Bhawan and RAAS to global brands like WelcomHotel ITC, Marriott, Novotel to mid-level brands like Lords Inn.

What to Buy:

Rajasthan is the best place to buy tie and dye fabrics. Cities like Jodhpur have shops which are usually called emporiums that house everything ethnic – from jewellery to paintings to home décor to fabric to sarees to home furnishings, et al.

Amritsar

∙●∙

On the Map:

Located just around 30 km from the Pakistan Border, Amritsar has always had a pious, religious significance for millions of Sikhs and Hindus across the world. It is home to the most revered Golden Temple (Harmandar Sahib), making it the religious and cultural centre of the Sikh Faith.

Flying Down:

Amritsar has an international airport and apart from being connected with all the major metros in India, it even has direct flights to the UK and Canada. By road, it has been connected since the British era by the Grand Trunk Road and there are many trains including Shatabdi (now the Vande Bharat) that connect it well with Delhi.

Moving Around:

The biggest attraction in Amritsar is undoubtedly the Golden Temple. It has such reverence that people from far and wide, of all faiths, come to visit and pay obeisance to Guru Granth Sahib. The Temple itself has intricately carved meenakari work on walls, a golden done and sports an architecture that is an amalgamation of Hindu and Islamic styles.

As in all Gurudwaras, there is free langar service of a vegetarian meal. P.S: The daal in langar is to die for, apart from the kada parshad.

Near the Golden Temple is the Akal Takht, which is one of the five seats of power for the Sikh religion. It is a beautifully built five-storied temple in white marble that reflects faith and belonging.

A must visit nearby is the Jallianwala Bagh, that evokes extreme emotions owing to the horrific incident that happened there during the British rule. You can pay your respects to the hundreds of innocent people killed there, at the memorial inside the garden.

Another religious place that has its significance and is most revered, is the Durgiana Temple. Located inside a small lake, the Temple has close resemblance to the Golden Temple and is definitely worth a visit.

A unique example of Indo-Saracenic architecture is the Khalsa College in Amritsar. It looks like a palace, with its sprawling gardens that resembles more like a royal abode than an educational institution. Another architectural gem in the city that should be in your itinerary is the Ram Tirath Ashram. The Temple inside the ashram has a big statue of sage Valmiki and it is believed that Luv and Kush were born here.

If you want to know more about the history of Punjab and its most illustrious ruler, Maharaja Ranjit Singh, visit the Gobindgarh Fort. Opened just a couple of years ago to the public, the Fort has a coin museum, exhibits warfare, has whispering walls (Kandha Boldiyan Ne) that showcases the Maharaja's life through a spectacular sound and light show.

Giving an adrenalin rush and arousing your patriotic feelings is the Wagah Border where every evening a ceremony of change of guards takes place. During the ceremony, one can witness both the Indian as well as the Pakistani side, singing, dancing to patriotic songs apart from the lowering of the flags of both countries and military exercises.

Stay in Comfort:

Being an important city of Punjab, you will find most branded hotel chains having a property in the city, like Radisson Blu, Best Western, Hyatt, Marriott, Ramada, Park Inn, Holiday Inn, Le Meridien, Sarovar Portico, Lemon Tree, etc. You will literally be spoilt for choice.

What to Buy:

Phulkari dupattas should be on the top of your list when you are in Amritsar. The best place to purchase these exquisite hand-embroidered pieces is the market outside the Golden Temple. Other items that Amritsar is famous for, is its papad and the Punjabi Wadi, which are sun dried; spiced lentil dumplings are also the speciality of Amritsar.

Jammu

•●•

On the Map:

The winter capital of the state of Jammu and Kashmir, Jammu has always been a transit point for thousands who flock to the Vaishno Devi Shrine at Katra, some 44 km away. But, slowly people are making a stopover in the city too, discovering its tourist potential. Situated on the banks of the River Tawi, Jammu is barely 1.5 hours away from the border with Pakistan. Earlier, it was not considered safe due to terrorism, but now that the state of J&K is experiencing fewer incidents of violence, it is completely safe to go there.

Flying Down:

Jammu is well connected with Delhi and Mumbai by air, though the rail network has always been strong. Apart from various express trains, even the recently launched Delhi-Katra Vande Bharat goes via Jammu. While departing from Jammu by air, passengers need to know that owing to the situation in the state, they need to report 3 hours before departure time as there is a three-level security that they would need to navigate.

Moving Around:

Apart from the time immemorial Vaishno Devi trek outside Jammu, the first place you must visit in the city is the famous Raghunath Temple. Including seven different shrines dedicated to various Gods and Goddesses, Raghunath Temple is located in the heart of the city, in the midst of a bustling market. It is considered to be one of the largest temple complexes in northern India.

After paying obeisance to the deities, head to the Bahu Fort, built on the banks of River Tawi. The fortress houses a temple of Goddess Kali and has sprawling, well-manicured gardens overlooking the river. Makes for a perfect day out for a picnic.

The other two palaces in the city are Amar Mahal and next to it is Hari Niwas Palace. While the former one is now a museum and tells you about the Dogra dynasty that ruled the state, the latter is now a heritage hotel. Amar Mahal is built like a French chateau and walks are also organised in its lawns telling visitors more about the history of the city. The museum showcases paintings by renowned artists like M.F. Husain and Laxman Pai.

Another palace that is a must-visit is the Mubarak Mandi Palace which served as the royal residence of the Maharaja of Jammu and Kashmir. It houses a Dogra Art Museum showcasing miniature paintings apart from other handicrafts from the area.

You must visit the Peer Kho Temple, a natural Shivling, just outside the city.

If you can spare a day extra on your trip for excursions, then go to the Mansar Lake, some 62 km away from Jammu. The view of the sparkling waters surrounded by lush greenery and mountains is truly breathtaking.

You can even take a one night trip to Patnitop near Udhampur, 122 km from Jammu. It is a stunning hill station frequented for trekking, outdoors, skiing and bathing in natural springs.

Stay in Comfort:

Jammu has a number of branded luxury hotels like Radisson Blu, Country Inn and Suites, Sarovar Portico, Lords Inn, Vivanta, Zone by the Park, etc. While I have stayed in Radisson Blu, which is at par with its other properties across India, one option that must be considered is KC Residency. Located at a walking distance from the Raghunath Temple, the rooms at KC Residency are plush to say the least. Being one of the oldest hotels in the city, its revolving restaurant on the top floor is extremely famous among locals.

What to Buy:

Jammu is one city that has a lot to offer in terms of shopping. You have Kashmir emporiums that sell Kashmiri artifacts like papier mache products, pashmina shawls, carpets, firans, etc. There are several showrooms in Gandhi Nagar that offer great designs and quality like Angad Creations.

You can also buy a number of nuts in the Raghunath Bazaar, next to the temple like ground nuts, cashew nuts, almonds, raisins, etc. Sweets made of nuts are also widely available. Jammu Rajma has been famous from time immemorial.

Gwalior

• • •

On the Map:

Located in the North of Madhya Pradesh, Gwalior has been famous in history for being the seat of the Scindia royal family. It is also close to Delhi, being just 300 km from the capital. Steeped in medieval ages, it is a must-visit for all those who like to delve into the annals of history.

Flying Down:

Gwalior has only recently come onto the aviation map of India. It now has direct flights to Delhi and Mumbai and a smaller flight to Indore. However, by rail and road, it is well connected to the Delhi-Mumbai route. I took the Gatiman Express from Gwalior to Delhi and in just 3 hours, reached my destination.

Moving Around:

Start your sightseeing in Gwalior with the towering Gwalior Fort. It looks down upon the Old City areas like a majestic elephant and when you drive up the winding road to the hilltop; you get a glimpse of what is in store for you above. At a particular point, after the road takes many twists and turns moving up the hill, there are Jain sculptures cut out of rocks that will take your breath away.

The space at the top is huge, to say the least. The Fort includes six palaces, rock-cut temples, spacious gardens, a museum, a school and residential quarters of people living there. Located inside the Fort complex is the uniquely named Saas Bahu Temple, dedicated to Lord Vishnu and Lord Shiva. The intricate carving of the temple will leave you awe-struck and due to it being situated atop a hill, you will get a mesmerising view of the city below.

To witness the lavish, opulent lifestyle of the Scindia royal family, one must visit the Jai Vilas Palace which houses a museum showcasing chandeliers, artefacts and furniture of the bygone era.

You can pay tribute to Tansen's Mausoleum and also visit the Gujari Mahal archaeological museum full of sculptures and artefacts dating back to the Gupta period. The palace was built by Man Singh Tomar for his beloved wife, Mrignayanee.

The Teli ka Mandir is another architectural marvel that you need to visit. Built in true Dravidian style, the temple is a perfect mix of North and South Indian architectural styles. The Sun Temple, designed on the theme of Konark Temple in Odisha, is another must-visit.

If you have one day extra, do visit the Madhav National Park in Shivpuri, some 120 km from Gwalior. The National Park has a wide variety of wildlife like leopards, wolves, deer, jackals, crocodile, etc. Another trip can be to the Bateshwar group of Temples in Morena district, 130 km from Gwalior. There are 200 temples built in the early Gurjara-Pratihara era, dedicated to Shiva, Vishnu and Shakti. Seeing such a big group of temples is a sight to behold!

Stay in Comfort:

Gwalior has options for everyone. You have the Taj Usha Kiran Palace Hotel which is a heritage property, all luxurious and opulent. Neemrana also has a luxury heritage property called Deo Bagh that is outside the city set amidst greenery. There is Radisson Blu, Park Inn by Radisson and Clarks Inn in terms of modern luxury.

What to Buy:

You can buy Madhya Pradesh's famous Chanderi and Maheshwari silk sarees, suits or fabric from saree shops in Gwalior apart from handicraft items, stone and lacquer work artefacts.

Bhubaneswar

• • •

On the Map:

The capital of the State of Odisha, Bhubaneswar is also called the Temple City of India, being home to some 500 ancient temples. The city itself dates back to the Kalinga times and has been an important centre for centuries. I have been here umpteen times and the best part of the city is that half of it is designed a la Chandigarh, while the other half is of a modern metropolis. A perfect amalgamation!

Flying Down:

Being the state capital, Bhubaneswar is well connected by air to all major cities of the country with direct flights. So is the case with rail as well. In terms of road, Bhubaneswar is located on the important Chennai-Kolkata national highway.

Moving Around:

Being an ancient city, there is a lot to see in Bhubaneswar. Starting with the famous Lingaraj Temple, an architectural marvel and probably the biggest tourist attraction in the city. A visit to Bhubaneswar is incomplete without paying obeisance at this Shiva Temple.

Other exquisitely designed temples to visit are the Rajarani Temple, Parasurameswara Temple, Brahmeswara Temple, Mukteswara Temple, Kedar Gauri Temple, Shri Ram Mandir, Anant Vasudev Temple among others. All the temples are great specimens of ancient temple architecture with beautiful carvings of Gods and Goddesses, well-maintained lawns giving a sense of tranquility and peace to the visitors.

Apart from temples, you can also visit the Odisha State Tribal Museum which will give you a glimpse into the history, lifestyle and culture of the 62 tribes that inhabit Odisha.

Located 7 km from the city are the Udaygiri and Khandagiri caves from the 2nd century BC. Carved into the two mountains by Jain monks centuries ago, out of the original 117 caves, around 33 can be seen. 18 are at Udaygiri and the remaining 15 at Khandagiri.

If you have a day to spare, then you must visit Puri and Konark, that are around 63 km away from Bhubaneswar. Puri is famous for the sacred Jagannath Temple and its beach, while Konark is world-renowned for the Sun Temple and the Konark Wheel.

Near the two pilgrim centres is located the art and crafts village of Raghurajpur. When you enter the village, you will be pleasantly surprised to see almost every house showcasing the handmade arts and crafts of Odisha, like Pattachitra paintings, masks, idols, toys, etc. The two main streets of the village are strewn with art, with most houses sporting murals on their facades, making the whole place look like a rich tapestry of art.

Stay in Comfort:

Bhubaneswar has many big brands like Trident, IHCL, ITC, Vivanta, Mayfair, Swosti that have been very popular for years. Mayfair Lagoon is a class apart. Other mid and budget friendly hotels too abound in the city, if budget is an issue.

What to Buy:

Pattachitra paintings, Sambalpuri sarees and kurtas. Odisha has plenty of art and craft to be brought home. Of course, you must buy the amazing sweet, Cheena Poda before boarding your flight (a kind of desi milk cake) as it lasts only 3-5 days.

Nellore

•●•

On the Map:

Located on the banks of Penna River and nestled amidst hills and lush greenery, some 173 km from Chennai, is Nellore, the fourth most populated city in Andhra Pradesh. It has always been an important religious and commercial centre owing to its proximity to the coast, being 25 km away from Mypadu Beach and a similar distance to the Krishnapatnam Port.

Flying Down:

The nearest airport to Nellore is Chennai and Vijaywada, both being around 173 km away. Nellore falls on the Chennai-Kolkata highway, hence coming via Chennai is a much more comfortable way of visiting the city. The Tirupati-Secunderabad Vande Bharat Express stops at Nellore, making it easy to travel to the city via Hyderabad or Tirupati if you fly down there.

Moving Around:

The Ranganatha Temple has to be the first go-to place in Nellore. Dedicated to Lord Ranganathaswamy, the Temple has seven gold pots decorated with huge mirrors. There is an Adala Mandapam, a hall that will leave you awestruck with its inlay work. Situated along the banks of the Pennar River, the temple has great religious significance, attracting hundreds of devotees daily.

Some 13 km from the city is the Narasimhaswamy Temple, built at the foothills and dedicated to the fourth incarnation of Lord Vishnu. Above this temple is another temple of Adi Lakshmi, which you can visit.

Ramalingeswara Temple is also a must-visit, located some 30 km from Nellore. It is dedicated to Lord Shiva and Goddess Kamakshamma and is designed like an architectural marvel.

25 km away is the famous Mypadu Beach on the Bay of Bengal. Not as crowded as other beaches in Visakhapatnam or Chennai, Mypadu is perfect for a sunset stroll in the cool breeze. It is unspoiled and clean, offering a spectacular view of the ocean waters beyond.

For nature lovers and birdwatchers, there is the Nelapattu Bird Sanctuary, located 83 km from Nellore, roughly around one hour and 20 minutes away. It is home to the spot-billed pelican, though you can see other varieties too like white ibis, storks, herons and little cormorants.

The island of Sriharikota, from where India sends its space missions, is also in Nellore district, 120 km from the city. However, tourists are only allowed to visit during scheduled rocket launches or with prior permission owing to the sensitive nature of the mission.

Stay in Comfort:

Being a small city, there are no branded hotels in Nellore. The city still has its share of comfortable three-star hotels. Some of them are D.R. Uthama, Minerva Grand and Yeshopark.

What to Buy:

For shopping, the best place to go to in Nellore is the Paturu village, 10 km from the city. It is renowned for handicrafts and handloom sarees and is a go-to place to visit if you are looking to buy Andhra Pattu sarees.

Belagavi

•●•

On the Map:

Belagavi is in the northernmost part of Karnataka, nestled amidst the Western Ghats. It is famous for the Belagavi Fort, Temples and Mosques. It is also the winter capital of Karnataka, with the assembly shifting to the newly built Vidhan Soudha every year for 10 days.

Flying Down:

Belagavi has direct flights to many metros like Delhi, Mumbai, Bengaluru, Hyderabad and Surat. By road, you can drive down from Kolhapur or better still Goa. In fact, the route from North Goa when it drives uphill the Western Ghats is probably the most scenic highways in India as it passes through the Chorla Ghat Nature Reserve crossing the hills and coming down into the plains at Belagavi.

Moving Around:

The Fort in Belagavi is its main attraction. Located in the city centre, the Fort is surrounded by a moat and was originally built in the 13th century by the Ratta dynasty. Initially, it had 108 Jain and 101 Shiva Temples which were subsequently destroyed in later invasions. Later dynasties added to the architectural splendor of the Fort by constructing more portions inside.

The Fort now houses the Military that has established its barracks there. You can enter through the narrow entrance where two temples dedicated to Lord Ganesha and Goddess Durga are located and then take a drive through lush lawns, Army quarters past ancient structures that give a glimpse of culturally rich bygone era.

In front of the Durga Temple is the Fort Lake that is beautifully lined with walkways and lush greenery, an ideal picnic spot for locals who come there every evening to spend time with family and friends.

After the Fort, head to the Kapileshwar Temple dedicated to Lord Shiva. It is believed that the darshan of the 12 Jyotirlinga's is incomplete if not started from Kapileshwar. The other temple you must visit is the Kamal Basti inside the Fort compound. A Jain Temple built under the Ratta dynasty, it is shaped like a lotus (hence the name) with the names of 24 Tirthankaras engraved on each petal. There is also the Military Mahadev Temple to visit, managed by the Indian Army, which is quite popular among locals and tourists alike.

If you have a day to spare, Belagavi is home to a few waterfalls like Gokak (50 km from city), Godchinamalakai (40 km) and Vajrapoha falls (31 km from city). Their cascading waters make for a great picnic spot where visitors can enjoy swimming or taking selfies of the shimmering waters and the hills beyond.

You can also visit the Yellur Fort, 11 km from Belagavi. It is situated atop a hill surrounded by a green countryside and has been ruled by Marathas, Hoysalas, Bahamanis, etc. The Fort has a Shiva Temple inside and it gives you a breathtaking view of the valley beyond.

Stay in Comfort:

Belagavi has two luxury hotels – Fairfield by Marriott and Mayur Belgaum Presidency. Three-star properties like Central, Hotel Sagittarius, Lords Eco Inn amongst others are also good.

What to Buy:

Khade Bazaar is the most popular market in Belagavi and has everything that one can imagine: apparel, jewellery, household items, gift stores, footwear and accessories.

Thrissur

..

On the Map:

Located in the middle of Kerala, an hour away from Kochi, Thrissur is known for the famous Thrissur Pooram festival, the most colourful temple festival in Kerala. It is also referred to as the cultural capital of the state.

Flying Down:

Since Thrissur is just 84 km away from Kochi, it is better to fly down to the commercial capital of Kerala and then drive down to Thrissur. Kochi is well connected to all the metros of India and even abroad, especially to countries in the Gulf and South-East Asia.

Moving Around:

Once you reach Thrissur, your first stop should be the famous and revered Vadakummnathan Temple dedicated to Lord Shiva, located in the centre of the city. In fact, when you drive along the road outside, you will realise that the Temple is actually like a roundabout, around which the city revolves.

The Temple is known worldwide as the place where the famous Thrissur Pooram festival is held every year in the months of April and May. The festival was the brainchild of the then Maharaja of Kochi, Shakthan Thampuran.

Thrissur Pooram sees temples in and around Vadakkummnathan take out processions with their deities perched atop traditionally attired elephants to Vadakkummnathan to pay obeisance to Lord Shiva. The festival ends with a spectacular display of fireworks. Such is the popularity of Thrissur Pooram that it draws nearly a million tourists every year, benefitting the tourism industry in the city and its neighbouring regions.

You ask anyone in Kochi what to see in Thrissur and the prompt reply would be Athirappally Waterfalls. It's not located in the city and is on the way from Kochi to Thrissur. A picnic spot for many in both cities, the waterfalls are a perfect place to explore the rich flora and fauna of the Western Ghats. Also referred to as the Bahubali Falls or even the Niagara Falls of India, Athirappally makes for a spectacular stopover en route to Thrissur.

There is a pool at the top before the water cascades down the mountain. You have to climb down 100 metres to get to the base of the gushing waters enjoying its spray and the cool breeze that comes along with it.

Other places to visit in Thrissur are the Vaddakkera Palace of the erstwhile Maharaja of Kochi, built in a mixture of Kerala and Dutch styles; Shankara Samadhi of Adi Shankaracharya; Basilica of Our Lady of the Dolores; Bible Tower seen from far and wide. Temples like the Arattupuzha dedicated to Lord Ayyappa, the Thiruvambadi Krishna Temple and the Triprayar Temple for Lord Rama are also some of the famous places in Thrissur.

If you have one day extra, you can visit the beaches of Snehatheeram, Vadanappally, Periyambalam, Munakkal and Nattika. Out of these, Snehatheeram is the most scenic beach on the Arabian Sea in Thrissur district.

Stay in Comfort:

While Thrissur has a Hyatt Regency, other properties are equally good like Hotel Dass Continental, Hotel Trichur Towers, The Garuda, White Palace Hotel, etc.

What to Buy:

You can buy Kerala handicrafts like Kathakali figures, paintings on bamboo, cotton and silk sarees, brass artefacts and yes… how can I forget, gold ornaments. Thrissur is the home of the renowned Kalyan Jewellers.

Vadodara and Bharuch

••

On the Map:

Situated in the Eastern part of Gujarat, Vadodara and Bharuch fall on the important Delhi-Mumbai industrial corridor. Bharuch, is an important industrial city along with its twin Ankleshwar, located across the Narmada River. The distance between Vadodara and Bharuch is around 78 km, hence have clubbed these two cities in one chapter as visiting both in one trip is very doable.

Flying Down:

Vadodara is well connected with all major metros like Delhi, Mumbai, Bengaluru and Hyderabad. The Ahmedabad-Vadodara expressway makes it convenient for those coming via Ahmedabad. Vadodara also falls on the Delhi-Mumbai expressway and once the expressway is functional, coming here by road will be a good option.

Moving Around:

The first place you must visit in Vadodara is the majestic Laxmi Vilas Palace, the private residence of the then Maharaja Sayyajirao Gaikwad III. It is supposed to be four times the size of the Buckingham Palace in London. The Palace compound has many buildings, one being the Maharaja Fateh Singh Palace which today is a museum that showcases paintings by celebrated artist, Raja Ravi Varma. The Palace is built in the Indo-Saracenic architectural style that is an amalgamation of Hindu, Gothic and Mughal styles.

The Sayyaji Gardens and the Ajwa Nimeta Garden are perfect for leisure walks in the afternoon or evening. The latter even sports a musical fountain that is a big draw with locals. The Sursagar lake in the middle of the city also makes for a leisurely evening out.

You can also visit the ISKCON Baroda and the BAPS Swaminarayan Temple to pay your respects to the deity plus admire the grandeur of temple architecture.

Other places to see in Vadodara are the Makarpura Palace, Sardar Patel Planetarium and the famous Maharaja Sayyajirao University.

If you have a day to spare, you can visit the Pavagadh Temple, dedicated to Mahakali, around 54 km from Vadodara. Located between the Panchmahal district and part of the Champaner-Pavagadh Archaeological Park, the Temple has been redeveloped and today attracts thousands of devotees on a daily basis.

Moving on to Bharuch, which is located on the Narmada River before it merges with the sea, the city can be accessed on a day's trip from Vadodara. The main tourist spots to see are the Narmada Park and the Nilkantheshwar Temple, which offers stunning views of the Narmada River. The Temple is dedicated to Lord Shiva and as the name suggests, worships the God in the form when he had kept poison in his throat during the Samudra Manthan.

As in most Gujarati cities, Bharuch also has a Swaminarayan Temple, made like all others as an architectural marvel. You can also go on a drive on the Golden Bridge over the Narmada River that connects Ankleshwar to Bharuch to see the Bridge which is built like a maze.

However, the place you must visit in Bharuch is the Kabirvad. Just 15 km from the city, Kabirvad is built on an island in the Narmada River and is named after Saint Kabir, who spent many years of his life here. It is approachable by a thrilling 10-minute boat ride from the Shuklatirth Shiva Temple on the shore. When I visited, the monsoon had just gotten over and the river was full of water, making the boat ride even more fulfilling.

On the island is a spectacular banyan tree grove that spreads over – hold your breath – a massive three kilometres. There is a temple for the Saint and just sitting under the huge grove will give you solace in just few minutes. Truly, a memorable experience.

Stay in Comfort:

Vadodara is home to Hyatt, Taj Vivanta, Ginger, Lemon Tree, Regenta, Sayyaji, Lords Inn, ITC, Grand Mercure, Fortune Inn – you name it and they are there.

What to Buy:

When in Gujarat, you must look out for Bandhni, ethnic ghagra-choli, mirror work clothes, silver jewellery, applique work, ethnic becovers, et al. You must try the local food like dhokla, fafda, dabeli, sev usal to get a real taste of the state.

Kota

•••

On the Map:

The third largest city in Rajasthan, after Jaipur and Jodhpur, Kota is situated in the southern part of the state on the banks of Chambal River. In the past decade, it has emerged as a leading coaching centre destination in India becoming home to lakhs of students from across the country.

Flying Down:

Kota is accessible by flight from Jaipur which is a good five hours away. However, the best way to visit the city is via train as Delhi has the Janshatabdi train to Kota and the city is en route with most trains going from North to South and vice versa. By road too, the connectivity is good as Kota is on the Delhi-Mumbai route.

Moving Around:

As you alight from the train and exit the railway station, the cleanliness of the city roads will surprise you. The drive inside the city over the flyovers will take you around the Chambal River, to enter into the new part that is full of apartment complexes, malls and multiplexes.

However, the biggest focal point of Kota remains the Chambal River and the riverfront that has been designed alongside it. The banks sport beautifully landscaped greens named as the Chambal Gardens, ideal for a stroll alongside the river.

Further down is the Kishore Sagar Lake, a man-made water body, built by the then Prince of Bundi. It has various attractions around it, a new one being the Seven Wonders Park, which has replicas of the Seven Wonders of the World in miniature form. You can see the Taj Mahal, Eiffel Tower, Egyptian Pyramids, Leaning Tower of Pisa, Statue of Liberty, etc. in their miniature forms and pose for photographs with them.

In the middle of the lake is the beautifully designed masterpiece, Jag Mandir. Used by the erstwhile royals for recreation, the place looks resplendent at night when lights illuminate it. It is approachable by boat and makes for a splendid evening out with family.

The Kota Barrage, a dam built on the Chambal River, is perfect for a day visit to see its shimmering waters and taking a stroll along its banks. The dam is also a heaven for bird watchers as they get to see different species flying over its waters.

A must visit is the Garadia Mahadev Temple, especially for its stunning views of the Chambal River. Perched atop a hill, you can see the river taking a turn, where it is surrounded by lush greenery.

Another temple worth visiting is the Godavari Dham Temple, dedicated to Lord Hanuman. There is also the Shivpuri Dham which is home to 525 shivlings.

Photography enthusiasts can take a drive on the Chambal Hanging Bridge or visit the City Palace to see its architectural grandeur.

Staying in Comfort:

Kota has many hotels for all categories, though only two branded properties namely the Country Inn and Suites by Radisson and Clarks Premier. Other properties worth mentioning are Nevaji Palace, Lotus Ananta Elite, Hotel Lilac, etc.

What to Buy:

Definitely the famous Kota Doria saree. A blend of silk and cotton, the Doria saree comes in beautiful and vibrant colours and is the most sought after item in the city for tourists. Shops selling sarees are everywhere but it is better to buy from the old city area.

Other items to buy are Rajasthani artefacts like woodwork, pottery and stone products, bangles, jewellery and paintings.

Prayagraj

•●•

On the Map:

Popular since time immemorial as the place where the Sangam of sacred rivers Ganga, Yamuna and Saraswati takes place, Prayagraj (earlier named Allahabad) has been a go-to place for the devout Hindus for centuries. Known as the Triveni Sangam, Prayagraj has rich religious and cultural significance. The city has also played a significant role in the freedom struggle of India, being home to the Nehru Family. Not to mention superstar Amitabh Bachchan.

Flying Down:

Having recently come onto the aviation map, Prayagraj is today connected by air to Lucknow, Delhi, Mumbai and Bengaluru. By road, the city has good connectivity to Varanasi, Kanpur, Ayodhya,

Lucknow and north Madhya Pradesh. Trains going from north to east make a stopover in Prayagraj, notable among them being the Vande Bharat Express from Delhi to Varanasi.

Moving Around:

The first place to visit in Prayagraj has to be the Triveni Sangam. A place of great religious significance for the Hindus, the Sangam hosts the revered Kumbh Mela every 12 years, an event that sees lakhs of pilgrims converging upon the city. You can take a boat ride on the Sangam either early in the morning or in the evening to enjoy the confluence of the rivers in pleasant weather.

On the boat ride at the Sangam, you can also see the Akbar Fort that is probably the largest fort ever built by Mughal Emperor Akbar. It looks mesmerising sitting on the banks of the Sangam.

Other places to visit in Prayagraj is the Khusro Bagh, which houses mausoleums of the family of Jehangir. The mausoleums have been made with intricate carvings and inscriptions flanked by well-manicured lawns on all sides, making for a pretty picture in the middle of a concrete jungle.

Prayagraj is also famous for being the home of the Anand Bhawan, where the Nehru family resided. The two-storied home has now been converted into a museum where you can see how the Nehru Family lived. Next to the Anand Bhawan is the Jawahar Planetarium that takes you into the celestial world of stars and planets.

You can also visit the Allahabad Museum inside the Chandrashekhar Azad Park which gives you a peek into the annals of Indian history.

To click a photograph of the Sangam during sunset, drive along the New Yamuna cable bridge for the most spectacular view.

Stay in Comfort:

Hotels that top the charts in Prayagraj are Hotel Kanha Shyam (arguably the best hotel in the city), Millennium Inn, Max Hotels, Kanha Residency and Grand Continental. To experience the history of the city, stay at Welcome Heritage's property Badi Kothi which will transform you into a bygone era.

What to Buy:

The Civil Lines area of Prayagraj is the best shopping street in the city. It houses all local and national brands of clothing, jewellery, electronics and interiors. Prayagraj is also known for its street food where you can have the sumptuous aloo tikki, chana chaat, dahi papdi, dal ladoo, etc.

Deoghar

• • •

On the Map:

Located in the western portion of the Santhal Parganas on the Ajay River in the Rajmahal Hills in Jharkhand, Deoghar is primarily famous for the Baba Baidyanath Dham, dedicated to Lord Shiva. One of the twelve Jyotirlingas in India, the city is a holy sacred place for Hindus.

Flying Down:

Recently having joined the aviation map in India, Deoghar is connected by air to Delhi, Patna, Ranchi and Kolkata as of now. The Janshatabdi Express connects it well with Kolkata and Ranchi while via road you can access it from Ranchi, Kolkata and Patna.

Moving Around:

When I visited Deoghar, there were very few hotels around and it had only just started becoming a tourist destination for many. Once you reach there, without doubt the first place to visit is the Baba Baidyanath Dham.

Painted in white, the whole temple complex comprises the main temple of Lord Shiva along with 21 other temples dedicated to various Gods and Goddesses. Considered to be one of the most sacred Jyotirlingas in the country, the temple complex is what runs the economy of the small city.

We hired a priest who escorted us from the hotel to the temple on foot, explaining the history en route. He took care of the entry, helped us with the darshan and was our tour guide in the temple complex, explaining the sanctity and importance of each temple.

The Temple is filled with devotees during the month of Shravan wherein the queue stretches outside the city.

Being a pilgrimage town, the other temples to visit in Deoghar are the Nandan Pahar, a Nandi Temple built atop a hill and the Naulakha Temple dedicated to Radha-Krishna. 10 km from Deoghar is the Tapovan Mahadev Shiva Temple, amidst a number of caves. One of the cave has a Shivling and is believed to be the place where Valmiki stayed for penance.

A must visit is the famous Basukinath Temple in Dumka district, located 41 km from Deoghar. It is believed to be the court of Lord Shiva with the Shiva and Parvati Temples built in front of each other. It is believed that Lord Shiva and Parvati meet each other in the evening everyday, hence access to devotees is restricted for that much time.

Stay in Comfort:

Though there are no branded properties in Deoghar, some notable local hotels are Geetanjali International, Mahadev Palace, Vioray Inn and Rudrakhs Inn.

What to Buy:

Deoghar itself might not have much to offer in terms of shopping except buying pedas as prasad for the Baidyanath Temple. But you can visit the main markets in the city in search of the famous Godda Tussar saree, an area that is close to Deoghar.

Guwahati

•••

On the Map:

Known as the Gateway to the Northeast, Guwahati is not just the Capital of Assam, but for centuries has been the most important city in the region. In fact, it is a city which connects all the states of the North-East and acts as the epicentre of the region. Guwahati is located on the banks of the mighty Brahmputra, with the Shillong Plateau on one side.

Flying Down:

Guwahati is well-connected by air with all major metros of the country. Rail and road infrastructure are also at par. Hence, to visit

Guwahati you have multiple options to choose from, depending on your budget.

Moving Around:

The biggest attraction in Guwahati for centuries has been the Kamakhya Temple. An epicentre of the Tantric cult, the Temple is one of the 108 Shaktipeeth's in India. It is believed that the womb of Sati fell on Nilachal and it is worshipped here in the Goddess form Kamakhya.

While driving up the hill to the temple, you can stop en route at a viewing point to see the beauty of the entire valley.

The famous Ambubachi Festival is celebrated every year at the Kamakhya Temple to celebrate the menstruation of the goddess. It attracts thousands of devotees daily and is the perfect time to visit the temple if you want to see it in its full glory.

The other temple to visit in Guwahati is the Purva Tirupati Balaji Temple. Built in a true South Indian architectural style, it is a replica of the Tirupati Temple, giving people a chance to pay obeisance without having to visit Tirupati.

The other big attraction in Guwahati is the mighty Brahmaputra River, that is the lifeline of the region and of Bangladesh. You can sit, take a walk or even take a boat ride on the river to witness its sheer might. There is a ropeway at Kachari Ghat that enables you to see the entire expanse of the river, its islands and the hills beyond.

You can also take a boat ride on the river to Umananda Island, the smallest river island in Brahmaputra. It is believed that Lord Shiva created this island for his wife Uma for her happiness. It is also known as the Peacock Island, as it is in the shape of the national bird.

There is also the Mahabahu Brahmaputra River Heritage Centre where you can sit, relax and soak in the river. The centre has on display boats and other paraphernalia associated with fishing. It also showcases the culture of Assam, be it musical instruments or textiles.

Around Guwahati and especially en route from the airport, you will find several freshwater lakes blooming with water lilies and lotuses. The biggest among them is the Deepor Beel, now a big weekend destination for locals and tourists alike.

Stay in Comfort:

Guwahati has many hospitality brands like Taj Vivanta, Radisson Blu and Novotel that offer luxurious comfort. Other budget brands like Ginger and Treebo are also there along with other homegrown brands and standalone hotels in a budget that suits everyone.

What to Buy:

Definitely, the Mekhla Chaddor, the three-piece Assamese saree. If you go to the Assam Emporium, you can even buy matching necklaces with each saree. Other things to buy in Guwahati are handmade bamboo artefacts, gamcha (shawl), dry snacks and bamboo pickles.

Coimbatore

• • •

On the Map:
Surrounded by the Western Ghats, Coimbatore is the second largest city in Tamil Nadu and is the gateway to the hill station of Ooty. It is located on the Noyil river and borders the state of Kerala. Coimbatore is also famous for being the location of the Adiyogi Shiva Bust built by the Isha Foundation of famous seer, Sadhguru.

Flying Down:
Coimbatore has direct connectivity to a number of metros in India such as Chennai, Mumbai, Delhi, Bengaluru and Hyderabad.

Recently, the Coimbatore-Chennai Vande Bharat Express has also started providing fast rail connectivity. By road, Coimbatore is well connected to Chennai, Bengaluru and Kerala.

Moving Around:

Since it was built in 2017, the Adiyogi statue at the Isha Yoga Centre has become a major attraction in Coimbatore. Located 24 km away from the city centre in the Velliangiri mountains of the Western Ghats, The Adiyogi Bust stands 112 feet tall and is carved out of 500 tonnes of steel.

I went in the morning after my early morning flight and the highway was lined with people selling cherries, a fruit that grows in the surrounding hills in the winter. When you reach the Adiyogi Bust, you will be completely awestruck. It looks gigantic and the setting of the hills in the background and fields around look like a film set.

A bullock cart takes you to the Adiyogi from the gate of the Isha Yoga Centre. You can even walk as it's just 10 minutes away. There is a canteen at the entrance that serves authentic and delicious South Indian cuisine and lots of ice cream kiosks on the way to the Adiyogi.

Other places to see in Coimbatore include a number of temples and waterfalls. Amongst the temples, the ones you should visit are the Marudhamalai Hill Temple towering at 500 feet; Velliangiri Hill Temple which is dedicated to Lord Shiva; Ayyappan Temple, located in the heart of the city and the Perur Pateeswarar Temple which looks resplendent on the banks of the river Noyyal.

For nature lovers, the area abounds with waterfalls, dams and nature reserves. Of note is the Niligiri Biosphere Nature Reserve which boasts thousands of species of flora and fauna. 63 km away is the Kodiveri Dam on the Bhavani River which has become a major weekend picnic destination for locals.

While the Vydehi Falls are 35 km away, the Suriveni Falls are 37 km from Coimbatore, However, if you have a day to spare, then you can visit the Monkey Waterfalls which is 65 km from the city and offer a spectacular location for a perfect family's day out.

Apart from temples and waterfalls, Coimbatore is also home to the Gedee Car Museum that showcases vintage cars from various countries in excellent condition. You can also visit the TNAU Botanical Garden which has many varieties of trees, shrubs, herbs and flowers.

There is also the Glass Forest Museum, located inside the premises of the Forest College Campus. The museum has a lot of replicas of wild animals stuffed to make them look real.

Stay in Comfort:

Being an important commercial centre of South India and located close to the textile city of Tiruppur, Coimbatore is home to all major hospitality brands of the country. Be it ITC, Vivanta, Le Meridien, Ibis, Zone by the Park and Lemontree coupled with leading local brands like The Residency, Gokulam Park and Hash Six.

What to Buy:

Like in most South Indian cities, the best things to buy here are brass artefacts and God figures, silk sarees, jewellery, etc., with the Gandhipuram market being the best place to buy this.

Udaipur

..

On the Map:

Popularly known as the City of Lakes, the city of Udaipur is located in the southern part of Rajasthan. Extremely sought after for weddings, especially among celebrities, Udaipur is an important tourist centre attracting lakhs of domestic and international visitors annually.

Flying Down:

Since it has always been a popular tourist city, Udaipur is well connected to Delhi and Mumbai. It also has flights to Bengaluru, Hyderabad, Jaipur, Ahmedabad and Indore. New expressways have connected it well to Delhi, Jaipur and Ahmedabad. Rail connectivity is very good with Udaipur being connected to all major junctions in Northern and Western India.

Moving Around:

There is so much to see in Udaipur. But if you are on a two-day trip, below are the places to visit.

Though Udaipur has a number of sprawling resorts, if you are visiting for the first time, try to stay along Lake Pichola. It gives a spectacular view and an old-world charm a la Europe. Start with a visit to the famous City Palace overlooking the lake. It gives you a glimpse into the grandeur of the Mewar royal family replete with ornate arches, gilded furniture, mirror halls, murals, marble work, etc. The sound and light show in the evening is also worth attending.

From one of the arches, you can see the famous and spectacular Lake Palace which is a heritage hotel run by the Taj Group. You can also see it on a boat ride in the Lake Pichola that will take you along all the heritage properties lining its waters.

Near the entrance of the City Palace is the Jagdish Mandir that is built in the Indo-Aryan style. Its black stone deity of Lord Vishnu and the brass Garuda are a sight to behold.

Elsewhere in the city, Saheliyon ki Baari is a garden you must visit. The place has manicured gardens blooming with flowers along with marble sculptures, fountains, pools and baithaks.

Other lakes in and around the city are the Fateh Sagar, Rajsamand, Doodh Talai, Jaisamand, Jiyan Sagar and Udaisagar. All are nestled amidst hills and greenery, adding to the beauty of Udaipur.

To get a better view of the famous Fateh Sagar lake, visit the majestic Sajjangarh Palace that overlooks it. Located atop a hill, the castle looks straight out of a fairy tale. The Monsoon Palace as it's called, is a perfect spot for taking pictures and making memories of a lifetime. You can take a boat ride on the lake to the island in the middle.

Other places to see in Udaipur are the Maharana Pratap Memorial overlooking the Fateh Sagar lake, the Vintage Car Museum to look at those old beauties, Bagore-ki-Haveli which is now a museum showcasing heirlooms, art pieces of the royal family and the Karni Mata Temple atop a hill, accessible via a ropeway. The ropeway will enable you to see Udaipur's lake beauty from the skies.

If you have a day to spare, visit the revered Nathdwara Temple, 45 km from Udaipur, dedicated to Shrinathji, a form of Lord Krishna. The Temple has been designed like a Rajasthani Haveli and has a series of courtyards that open into the main sanctum sanctorum.

Stay in Comfort:

In Udaipur, you will be spoilt for choices in terms of hotels. There are luxury resorts nestled amidst the Aravalli's, luxury hotels on the banks of the Lake Pichola, heritage hotels and business hotels. I stayed in a haveli-turned-hotel on the Lake Pichola called Amet Haveli, whose location is to die for. Its restaurant, Ambrai, is famous for its food and the open-air setting on the banks of the lake overlooking the City Palace in all its glory. The night view is stunning, to say the least.

What to Buy:

Tough to list all items as what not to buy in Udaipur! You have souvenirs like Rajasthani puppets; stuffed horses; tie and dye fabrics like scarves, tops, sarees; mirror work ghaghras; silver jewellery; leather diaries; wooden and ceramic sculptures; bedsheets, etc.

Udaipur is also home to the Nathdwara miniature paintings that you will find all over the heritage area of Lake Pichola.

Ujjain

•••

On the Map:

Located in the western part of Madhya Pradesh in the Malwa region, Ujjain has been an important pilgrim centre for centuries. The Ardh Kumbh takes place here every 12 years on the banks of the Shipra River and the Mahakal Jyotirlinga is the mainstay of the local economy there.

Flying Down:

Being an hour away from Indore, Ujjain is easily accessible by road if you take a flight to Indore. Indore is well connected to all major metros like Delhi, Mumbai, Ahmedabad, Hyderabad, Bengaluru, Kolkata and Chennai. Rail connectivity is excellent as the city is directly connected to all regions of the country.

Moving Around:

Without doubt the first stop in Ujjain has to be the Mahakaleshwar Temple. One of the 12 Jyotirlingas in the country, Mahakaleshwar Temple, has been built with influences of the Maratha and Chalukya empires.

The idol at Mahakaleshwar is south-facing, a unique aspect of the Temple. Its Bhasma Arti is very famous and attracts thousands of devotees from across India on a daily basis. Before you enter the temple complex, it would be a good idea to get your forehead smeared with trishul or other elements associated with Lord Shiva. You will find young boys and girls en route to the temple offering these services for a small fee.

Recently, the whole temple complex has been restructured and the Mahakal Lok that has been designed all around is definitely worth a visit.

The Mahakal Lok contains 108 stambhs of Lord Shiva depicting the Tandav Swaroop of the God. The area is full of sculptures and murals pertaining to the life of Lord Shiva all along the Mahakal Path leading up to the temple. There is a plaza that has a pond with Lord Shiva's statue in its middle, along with fountains.

A must-visit after Mahakaleshwar is the Kaal Bhairav Temple, who is said to be the most important of all the eight Bhairav's.

Other Temples to visit are the Ram Mandir with its ghats where the Kumbh Mela takes place every 12 years, Harsiddhi Temple of

Maa Annapurna, Birla Temple, the ISKCON Ujjain Krishna Temple and the Mangalnath Temple.

Apart from temples, there are some other places you can visit in Ujjain too. They include the Jantar Mantar, Vikram University and the Pir Matsyanendranath. The latter is located on a small lake and is in remembrance of one of the greatest leaders of the Nath sect of Saivism.

Stay in Comfort:

Though most devotees live in Indore and visit Ujjain on a day visit, due to a number of branded hotels in Indore. There are some local brands in Ujjain that offer a comfortable stay. Some notable ones are Hotel Abika Elite, Shipra Residency, Kalpana Palace, Hotel Imperial Grand, etc.

What to Buy:

To spend some extra time in the city, you can move around the market around Mahakaleshwar and buy short length kurtas, ladies suits, dupattas with Mahakal written over them. There are a number of shops selling puja items and souvenirs associated with Lord Shiva that you can take back as memories.

Darbhanga

•••

On the Map:

Located in the northern part of Bihar, Darbhanga has always been famous in history for its flamboyant Maharaja Kameshwar Singh Goutam Bahadur and his fleet of vintage cars. An important city in the Mithila region of the state, Darbhanga is called the cultural capital of Bihar, with the city being the centre of music, art, folklore and literary traditions in Sanskrit, Hindi and Maithili.

Flying Down:

Owing to the UDAAN scheme, Darbhanga is also on the aviation map of India and has direct flights from Delhi, Mumbai, Kolkata, Hyderabad and Bengaluru. By road, Darbhanga is connected to the nearby cities of Samastipur, Muzaffarpur, Sitamarhi and Madhubani. Rail connectivity too is good enough for people to reach the city.

Moving Around:

You can start your tour of Darbhanga with a drive in and around the Darbhanga Fort. One of the biggest historical sites in North Bihar, the Fort has been designed on the lines of Fatehpur Sikri. Hued in red, the Fort includes the Rambagh Palace and Nagrona Palace. Successors of the royal family still live in a part of its precincts. The Fort complex also houses the Kankali Temple.

The area in and around the Fort is full of small water bodies that add a refreshing feel to the whole place.

The grounds of the Narayan Mithila University are home to the famous Shyama Kali Temple. Built in 1933, the Temple – also hued in red – is believed to have been built on the ashes of the Maharaja of Darbhanga. The Temple has six temples in the complex, built around a pond that has been filled with water from seven rivers. The whole complex gives a very peaceful, soulful feeling that emanates a positive energy.

Ahilya Asthan is located in a village near Darbhanga called Ahilya Gram, dedicated to the wife of the Sage Rishi. She was transformed from stone to living flesh when Lord Rama's feet touched the stone. The village gets a number of devotees on Ram Navami and it is celebrated with great fervour.

Chandradhari Museum is a perfect place if you want to know more about the history of the place. The museum, located on the Mansarovar Lake, showcases rare artefacts in stone, wood and clay as well as coins and precious gems and stones. Brass statues of Buddha and various gods and goddesses plus rare paintings on Ramayana and Geet Govinda are available there.

If you have a few hours extra, head to the Kusheshwar Asthan Bird Sanctuary comprising 14 villages where the land is waterlogged. Thereby making it a haven for birds. In the winter months, you can see the Siberian Crane, Pelicans, Bar-headed Goose and many more.

Stay in Comfort:

Five minutes from the airport is Hotel Garcia International, purportedly the best hotel in Darbhanga today. Others that can be considered are the Imperial Hotel, Grand SM Regency, and Hotel GV Heritage.

What to Buy:

Most definitely sarees, kurtas, bedcovers, stoles, fabrics in hand-painted Madhubani art. There are no showrooms for this. You will have to go to the homes of artists who have stocks available. Highly recommended is Padma Shri Asha Jha's studio, which has uniquely designed sarees, stoles and paintings. Men's kurtas can be made to order.

Mangaluru

On the Map:

The second largest city in Karnataka, Mangaluru is in the Dakshina Kannada area of the state with the Arabian Sea on one side and the Western Ghats on the other. Mangaluru is also a major port and an industrial hub in the country. It is also the epicentre of Tulu Nadu, a region which comprises Dakshin Kannada and Udupi in Karnataka and Kasaragod in Kerala, where people speak Tulu, a language that is a mix of all four languages of South India.

Flying Down:

Mangaluru has direct flights to Delhi, Mumbai, Bengaluru, Hyderabad, Chennai and Kochi. Being an important port, many highways pass through the city making travelling accessible. Similar is the case with rail connectivity.

Moving Around:

Mangaluru is a fascinating mixture of culture and natural beauty. Here you have the lush greenery of the Western Ghats on one side and the scenic beaches on the other. In fact, from the flight itself, you will see verdant greens extending right up to the sea. The tabletop runway at the Mangaluru airport is also unique as very few such runways exist in the world.

The drive from the airport to the city winds its way downhill and as you enter the city, the first thing that strikes you is the cleanliness. Entire stretches of roads are cemented, pedestrian pathways are paved and there is no litter anywhere.

Starting with the seashore first, some of the popular beaches at Mangaluru are Panambur, Ullal and Tannirbhavi. The beaches are located a few kilometers from the city and are next to the Mangalore Port. Panambur is the closest to the New Mangalore area and is located next to a steel plant. The beach is popular among locals, hence there are more crowds but also facilitates water sports as well.

Ullal and Tannirbhavi, in comparison, are quieter, much cleaner and more pristine. You can witness the sunset here against the horizon, making memories of a lifetime.

One of the most popular temples in recent times in Mangaluru is the Kudroli Gokarnath Temple. Dedicated to Lord Gokamanatha, a form of Lord Shiva, the Temple was built in 1912. Built in true Dravidian style, Gokarnath Temple has a seven-storey gopuram, adorned with sculptures of various Gods and Goddesses. In the temple courtyard too, there are statues of Nandi and a chariot. The Temple plays a major role in the famous Mangaluru Dasara.

Another famous and ancient temple is the Kadri Manjunath Temple. Built in 1068 AD, the temple is dedicated to Lord Shiva and is said to be the oldest Shiva Temple in the area. It has an eye-catching indigo-hued gopuram, adorned with sculptures of Gods and Goddesses in gold.

You can also visit the Sultan Battery built by Tipu Sultan to monitor ships coming into the Gurpur River. There is also the St. Alosyius Chapel set atop the Lighthouse Hill that has regal interiors and commands a majestic view of the sea.

Other places to visit are the Kadri Park which has a number of wild animals and birds in its conservatory; the Mangladevi Temple dedicated to a form of Goddess Durga; the Kateel Durgaparameshwari Temple; the Thousand Pillar Jain Temple and the Seemanthi Bai Government Museum that houses everything related to the region's history under its roof.

Stay in Comfort:

There are many brands that have set up shops in Mangaluru, namely Vivanta, Ginger, and Goldfinch. Apart from these, other hotels that provide luxurious stays are Avatar Hotel, Moti Mahal, Ocean Pearl, Hotel Sea View, etc.

What to Buy:

Mangaluru is known for its spices, coffee and nuts, which you can find in almost every market. Apart from that, Karnataka silk sarees at numerous saree showrooms is worth a buy.

A piece of advice: Do not leave Mangaluru without trying the Manguluru Bun and the famous Gadbad ice cream!!

Surat

•••

On the Map:

An important commercial city located in the South of Gujarat, Surat is on the Tapti River and is 30 km from the Gulf of Khambat. It is the epicentre of the textile industry and is also known as the Diamond City, being an important diamond cutting and polishing centre. Nearly 90% of the cutting and polishing of diamonds globally takes place in Surat.

Flying Down:

Surat has direct connectivity to many cities in India such as Delhi, Mumbai, Goa, Indore, Jaipur, Belagavi, Hyderabad, Bengaluru, Chennai and Kolkata. It is strategically located on the Delhi-Mumbai Expressway and any train that goes to Mumbai from Delhi or North India passes through Surat.

Moving Around:

Whenever I visit Surat, the first thing that strikes me as I drive from the airport into the city is its richness. The city looks as if there is money all around – which gives you a luxurious feel!

It is also the city of flyovers. After the plague in 1994, Surat went through a sea change in terms of cleanliness and infrastructure. Today, it has flyovers crisscrossing the city, making it easier for commuters to travel, plus it has become one of the cleanest cities in India.

Start your tour of the city with a visit to the famous Ambaji Temple located on the banks of the Tapti River. On the river is also the Sarthana Nature Park that is home to a number of wild animals and birds. It is a good picnic spot for families.

Nearby is the Jagdish Chandra Bose Aquarium, India's first multi-disciplinary aquarium that houses over 100 species of marine life plus a dolphin pool. You can also visit the Science Centre that has a museum, art gallery, planetarium and an amphitheatre.

As in all Gujarat cities, the Swaminarayan Temple is the most famous religious spot in the city. In terms of heritage, visit the Surat Castle that sits on the banks of the Tapti and served as a defence against foreign invasions.

A visit to the Tapti riverfront in the evening to see the sun setting against the river is truly mesmerising. You can also visit the Sneh Rashmi Botanical Garden to look at the various species of flora and fauna.

Being close to the sea, Surat has beaches nearby, that are a must-visit. The most famous among them is Dumas, some 18 km from the city frequented in large numbers by locals. The famous Dandi beach, which is made famous by Mahatma Gandhi for the Salt Satyagraha, is nearly 30 km from Surat. Suvali Beach near the industrial town of Hazira is also a beach you can consider going to.

The Gavier Lake in the city is a bird watcher's paradise and is a wonderful place to catch a breath of fresh air amidst nature in a busy city. You can also visit the Gopi Talav in the late evening to see its waters shimmer in the nite.

Not to forget, the recently opened Diamond Bourse, the largest office building in the world is worth a dekho while on the way to the airport.

Stay in Comfort:

There was a time when I only had the option of Lords Inn to stay in Surat. Located near the railway station, the hotel for years was the only business hotel, the city had. But, today Surat has hotels like Park Inn by Radisson, Marriott, Courtyard by Marriott and Le Meridien.

What to Buy:

What not but of course, textiles and diamonds. You will find numerous shops in the various textile markets in Surat selling fabrics, sarees from as low as Rs 100. Diamonds, though come at their own price!

You can also buy the famous Gujarati snacks like khakhra, thepla, gathiya from various food stores across the city. Do not forget to have dabeli and Surat's very own snack, locha before leaving the city.

Bikaner

• • •

On the Map:

A border district in Rajasthan, Bikaner is a city full of history, culture and architecture. Located in the Thar Desert, the city is named camel country and is home to the world's largest camel research and breeding centre. Around the city are many dunes apt for camps and safaris.

Flying Down:

Bikaner only has one flight from Delhi. Most people visit the city by taking a road trip from Jodhpur which has flights connecting it to various metros in the country. The highways are good and pass through the desert area, making it a nice journey to undertake. Rail connectivity too is good if you want to come here by train, especially via Jaipur.

Moving Around:

The city is a repository of beautifully styled palaces, forts and havelis, giving you a glimpse of its rich historical and cultural heritage. The biggest example of that in Bikaner is the Junagarh Fort. The grand structure built in the desert was completed in the 16th century and is a perfect example of Rajput and Mughal architectural styles.

The Fort includes palaces, gardens, balconies, jharokhas, etc, and represents 16 rulers since its inauguration including design elements from various generations as the centuries passed.

The other palace to see is the Lallgarh Palace which now serves as a heritage hotel. Constructed for Maharaja Ganga Singh in the early 20th century, the palace sports a European look and also houses the Sri Sadul Museum, showcasing memorabilia of the royal family from an era gone by.

Another palace worth visiting is the Laxmi Vilas Palace, which with its stunning design attracts tourists from far and wide. It too now functions as a heritage hotel.

Gajner Palace, built on the banks of the Gajner Lake, was initially built as a hunting lodge for Maharaja Ganga Singh. Built in true Rajput style, the Palace which too is now a hotel, offers myriad activities like desert safari, bird watching and other sporting activities.

Another historical place to visit is the Rampuriya Haveli which looks stunning, to say the least. Serving as abodes of wealthy businessmen in those times, the Haveli coupled with others like Rikhji Bagri ki Haveli, Haveli of Bairondon, Daga Chowk Haveli and the Sampatlal Agarwal Haveli, impart a feeling of grandeur to the old Bikaner area; as well as unique and spectacular insta stories.

A visit to Devi Kund and the royal cenotaphs is a must if you want to see architecture at its best. The cenotaphs are basically chatris that have been designed intricately to serve as the cremation ground for Bikaner's royal family.

Apart from palaces, one place that Bikaner has become synonymous with over the years is the famous Karni Mata Temple. The Temple is built with white marble and is a place of worship where rats play an important role. The Temple has around 25,000 black rats and these rats are worshipped as representative of the Goddess.

Other temples to visit in Bikaner are the exquisite Bhandasar Jain Temple dedicated to the fifth Tirthankara; the Kodamdesar Temple, built by the founder of Bikaner, Rao Bikaji, for an incarnation of Lord Shiva; Sri Lakshminath Temple dedicated to Lord Vishnu and Goddess Parvati and Kolayat, some 40 km from Bikaner, that is supposed to be the place where Kapil Muni meditated for peace and harmony.

The National Research Centre on Camels too now finds itself on the tourist map of Bikaner. Tourists can see different breeds of camels up, close and personal at the centre and even can feed them. Bikaner is also famous for its Camel Festival, that occurs in January every year. It includes camel races and camel dance as its main attraction.

The Sursagar Lake in the middle of the city is a famous picnic spot for locals in the evening where they can relax along its banks that sports a beautiful Shiva statue in the middle.

Stay in Comfort:

Full of heritage hotels, Bikaner has some outstanding properties to look out for like the Narendra Bhawan, Brij Gaj Kesri, Lallgarh Palace, Laxmi Vilas Palace, Vesta Bikaner Palace and a number of desert camps and resorts that are ideal for desert safaris.

What to Buy:

Bikaner is famous for artefacts, purses and jackets made from camel hide. Alternatively, you can also buy mojaris, lacquer bangles, bandhni dupattas and fabrics, kundan work, wooden antiques et al.

Raipur

•●•

On the Map:

I have been visiting Raipur for the past 10 years and the city has grown in size, scale and importance over the years. Previously a part of Madhya Pradesh, Raipur literally came into its own when the state of Chhattisgarh was formed in the year 2000. It is located in Central Chhattisgarh and is today an important regional industrial and commercial destination.

Flying Down:

Today, all major metros are connected to Raipur via flight, be it Kolkata, Delhi, Mumbai, Hyderabad, Bengaluru or Chennai. The highways are good and a new expressway from Raipur to Visakhapatnam is under construction and will further boost connectivity to the city. Rail network is superb and all major east, south and central bound trains make a stop at Raipur.

Moving Around:

As you drive from the airport to the city, the one thing that will strike you is lush greenery and a huge number of ponds that you will see around. In fact, in the whole of Chhattisgarh you will find ponds every few kilometres, probably the largest any state has in the country. All thanks to the abundant rainfall that the state receives.

Near the airport is the Naya Raipur area where the Central Park is a delight to see. Decorated with sculptures depicting tribal life, the park is perfect for a stroll in the evening, when it is lit up in light. Also at Naya Raipur is the Nandan Van Zoo which has a large variety of flora and fauna to see.

Another place to see the rich culture of Chhattisgarh is the Purkhauti Muktangan. It is a garden that showcases folk art, larger-than-life tribal sculptures and artefacts, all nicely woven in its green tapestry.

In the heart of the city is the Telibandha Lake which has been redesigned to include pedestrian walkaways, benches and graffiti on walls to make it look appealing. Called the Marine Drive of Raipur, the lake is an ideal evening getaway from the hustle and bustle of the city.

Ahead of the Telibandha Lake is the Gandhi Udyan Park that extends to the Bhagat Singh Chowk. It is a favourite haunt of locals who throng to the green area with family to spend their leisure time.

Raipur also has its own ISKCON Temple that looks as resplendent as its sister temples across India. Other temples to visit in and around the city are the Shadani Durbar, Mahamaya Temple, the Kevalya Dham Jain Temple and the Rajiv Lochan Temple.

Located 85 km from the city is the biggest waterfall in Chhattisgarh called the Ghatarani Waterfall. The waterfall has a breathtaking visual and is approachable after taking a small trek through the forest. At the bottom of the waterfall is a pool where you can swim and soak in the falls during summer.

Stay in Comfort:

There was a time when Raipur had its homegrown brands in the hospitality sector like the Babylon Hotel. But today, the city is home to various big and small international brands like Hyatt, Courtyard by Marriott, Sayyaji, Clarks Inn, Sarovar Portico, etc.

You can also explore the Mayfair Lake Resort, some 25 km from the city which offers stunning lakefront views amidst luxurious accommodation.

What to Buy:

Most definitely the exquisite Dokra art pieces like sculptures and other artefacts, made by tribals in the state. It is available in the state emporium and is a must-takeaway from Raipur. You will even see life-size sculptures of the same at the departure and arrival sections of the Raipur Airport. Other things to buy are terracotta products, stone sculptures, wrought iron items or the Kosa silk saree that is originally from the Raigarh district in Chhattisgarh.

Rajamahendravaram

• • •

On the Map:

Located just above the head of the delta of the Godavari River, Rajamahendravaram (previously known as Rajahmundry) is at the centre of the Godavari districts on the left bank of the river. It is also known as the cultural capital of Andhra Pradesh and its name has been derived from Rajaraja Narendra, the ruler of Chalukya dynasty of the 11th century who ruled over the city.

Flying Down:

Rajahmahendravaram has a small airport that connects it to Hyderabad, Bengaluru and Chennai and people from other cities can take connecting flights from here to the city. The highway from

Hyderabad is well established, while coming via Visakhapatnam is another alternative route. It is well connected by trains connect with all major cities in the South from where you can find connectivity to other parts of the country.

Moving Around:

The first and foremost place to visit in Rajamahendravaram is the ghat area along the Godavari River. As you alight from your cab at the roundabout with the proverbial, I love Rajamahendravaram board and walk into the ghat area, the whole area gives you a very vibrant and pleasant feel.

The ghats are well made. You can easily sit there, and relax while looking at the gushing waters of the river. You can see bridges on both side of the river – one is the Godavari Bridge which is a truss (rail-cum-road) bridge, while the older one is Havelock Bridge, used for rail still exists. New bridges have also been added, namely the Godavari Arch Bridge, built to replace the Havelock Bridge. The latest to be added is another truss bridge called the Godavari Fourth Bridge.

Near the Ghat is one of the oldest temples in Rajamahendravaram, named the Markandey Swamy Temple dedicated to Lord Shiva. It sits a little below the road level and is typically built in the Gopuram style, with beautiful sculptures of Gods and Goddesses.

Nearby is the famous ISKCON Temple, the second largest in South India after the one in Bengaluru. Built along the banks of the river, it is definitely worth a visit.

Located on the east bank of the Godavari is the Draksharamam, Temple dedicated to Lord Shiva. It is one of the five most important temples dedicated to Lord Shiva in the country.

The city also has the Sir Arthur Cotton museum, who was instrumental in forming the irrigation system from the Godavari River to help the farmers in the adjoining districts.

Around the city there are many places to go to. 40 km away is Pattiseema, a village surrounded by the lush greenery of the Papikondalu hill range, with the river meandering in between. It makes for a picturesque setting, ideal for your insta page.

Maredumili is an eco-tourism spot 80 km from Rajamahendravaram, famous for its ravines, water bodies, hills and green surroundings. At a similar distance, albeit on a different route, is Annavaram, known for its temple for Lord Vishnu. The village is located on the river Pampa and makes for a perfect picnic next to the waters.

Stay in Comfort:

Mostly homegrown brands are there in Rajamahendravaram, except for Sarovar Portico, which is an all India chain of 4-star hotels. Other hotels where you can expect a comfortable stay are Hotel Anand Regency, La Hospin, Hotel Shelton and River Bay.

What to Buy:

You can buy brass and wooden artefacts from various antique shops and shops selling puja items. Rajamahendravaram is famous for the Putharekulu, which is a wafer of thin starched rice paper filled with sugar, nuts, and dry fruits. You can also bring home the Palakova which is basically a doodh peda and the best place to buy it in the city is Gangaraju.

Tiruchirappalli

∙●∙

On the Map:

One of the most famous temple cities of India, Tiruchirappalli sits exactly in the centre of Tamil Nadu. The city is located on the River Cauvery. Uraiyur which was the capital of the Early Cholas from 3rd Century BC to 3rd Century AD, is a suburb of Tiruchirappalli. The city is known for the Srirangam Ranganathaswamy Temple, which is the largest functioning Hindu temple in the world, attracting pilgrims from far and wide.

Flying Down:

Trichy, as Tiruchirappalli is called colloquially, has an international airport and is connected domestically to Chennai, Bengaluru, Mumbai and Hyderabad with direct flights. The highways leading to Trichy are as good as it gets, while rail connectivity is at par too.

Moving Around:

The first place to visit in Trichy has to be the Sri Rangaswamy Temple located in the Srirangam area in the city. The economy of the city revolves around this 156-acre architectural marvel. The Temple is dedicated to Lord Ranganathswamy, a reclining form of Lord Vishnu. Incidentally, Lord Ranganthaswamy was the kuldevta of Lord Rama's family.

The Temple is like a city in itself and has 21 tower gates called the gopurams. It has 81 shrines and 39 pavilions making it the largest functioning Hindu temple in the world. It is a sight to behold with its intricate stone carvings, gopurams, sculptures and the entire edifice. You can easily spend 1-2 hours there.

As you drive around the city, you will see a rock towering above the skyline with a fort built atop it. It is the Tiruchirappalli Rock Fort that was fortified by the Vijayanagar Empire and is a witness to several battles in history involving the Marathas, Bijapur's Adil Shah, Madurai's Nayak and the British in various centuries.

The Fort has three main temples – the Manakka Vinayakar temple, the Ucchi Pillayar Temple and the Taayumaanavar Koyli Shivastalam. There are two rock-cut temples known as the Upper Cave and Lower Cave Temples.

The Rockfort Ganpathi Temple (the Manakka Vinayakar) encompasses the rock that is supposed to be the oldest in the world.

The Temple has two parts – the Thayumanaswamy dedicated to Lord Shiva and Pillayar dedicated to Lord Ganesha. You can see the entire city, the Srirangam Temple and the Cauvery River from the Temple's terrace.

Other temples you can visit include the Thiruvanaikoil Temple and the Vekkal Amman Temple dedicated to Goddess Parvati. The former is located on an island with the Cauvery and Coleroon rivers surrounding it. It is one of the Panchabhoota Temples, representing the element water.

Apart from temples, there are two dams that one can visit. They are the Kallanai Dam and the Mokkumbo. Both are picnic spots for the locals and make for a good evening out.

If you have the time, you can also visit the Puliyancholai Waterfalls, some 41 km from the city at the Koli Hills. The falls are very popular and attract many tourists.

Stay in Comfort:

There are two hotels in Trichy that are perfect for a luxurious stay – the Courtyard by Marriott and the SRM Hotel. There are other options in the budget category that you can opt for.

What to Buy:

There are a lot of crafts from Tamil Nadu that you can pick up from Trichy – stone carvings, brass artefacts, bamboo items, paintings, pottery, jewellery and metal ware.

Kozhikode

On the Map:

Kozhikode, previously known as Calicut, is a major city in Kerala located on the Malabar Coast. The port city has since time immemorial been an entry point into Southern India for the Chinese, Persians, Dutch, Portuguese, French and British. It is near Kozhikode at Kappad Beach that Vasco Da Gama landed in 1498.

Flying Down:

Kozhikode is connected to Bengaluru, Kochi, Chennai, Hyderabad, Mumbai and Delhi via direct flights and flights to the Gulf. Recently, two new Vande Bharat trains have been launched that stop at Kozhikode as well and cut through Kerala. By road, the city is well connected to other cities in Kerala namely Kochi and Kannur, as well as to Bengaluru and Coimbatore across the Western Ghats.

Moving Around:

The Kozhikode airport is in the adjoining district called Malappuram and it takes nearly an hour to reach the city. However, you will find the whole route full of lush greenery, as is usually the case when you travel anywhere around the Western Ghats from Mumbai to Kerala.

However, what is different here are the backwaters. You will encounter one before entering the hustle and bustle of the city. Your first drive through the city will take you to its fulcrum – the Mananchira Square, which is an artificial pond in the middle of the city from where roads lead in all directions.

The Square was built in the 14th century by the then Zamorin Mana Vikrama as a bathing ghat. The pond and the adjoining garden space are now a favourite recreational place for the locals.

The other place to visit is the Tali Temple, one of the oldest temples in the region. The Temple is dedicated to Lord Shiva and is built in true Kerala courtyard style with a pond preceding it. The pond area with its beautiful monuments makes for an eclectic view in the night when lights lit up the entire area.

The other ancient temple one can visit is the Azhakodi Devi Temple, dedicated to Bhadrakali. Other temples are the Varakkal Temple and the Valayanad Temple.

Near the city is the beautiful Kallai River and the Canoli Canal, which were earlier busy ports during the colonial rule till the new one was built in Independent India.

Not to miss is an evening stroll on the promenade on Kozhikode Beach, perfect for its sunset. The other beaches which are around Kozhikode that one must visit are Beypore Beach (which has a floating bridge) which is 11 km from the city; the Thikkoti

Lighthouse 31 km away, located on a rocky shore; Kappad Beach which is 16 km away where Vasco Da Gama landed in 1498 and the Parappally Beach 24 km away, famous for its palm trees and sandy stretch.

If you have a day to spare, you can visit the beautiful Kozhippara Falls that are around 50 km from Kozhikode. They provide a stunning view of cascading waters set amidst green and rocky surroundings. Other waterfalls near the city are Thusharagiri Waterfall that cascades from three different directions and Orakuzhi fall, located near the Kakkayam dam. Peruvannamuzhi Dam also makes for a picturesque setting.

For bird watchers there is the Kadalundi Bird Sanctuary around 20 km from the city that has over 100 species of bird and marine life.

Stay in Comfort:

Kozhikode has two hotels of the well-known Kerala brand Raviz – one is The Raviz inside the city and the other is The Raviz Kadavu on the airport road on the backwaters. Taj has set up The Gateway and there are other hotels like Tripenta, Dimora, Park Residency, Keys Select and Malabar Palace, that are good options too.

What to Buy:

Sweets from SM Road, Calico Cotton, rosewood artefacts, the Koyilandy hookah, and the usual souvenirs from Kerala like the Kathakali face and Radha-Krishna paintings made on bamboo.

Chhatrapati Sambhaji Nagar

•••

On the Map:

Renamed after the illustrious son of Chhatrapati Shivaji Maharaj, Chhatrapati Sambhaji Nagar (earlier called Aurangabad) is located in a hilly region in the Deccan Plateau. The city is the gateway to major tourist attractions like the Ajanta and Ellora caves, the Grishneshwar Jyotirling, Bibi Ka Maqbara (built on the lines of the Taj Mahal) and various monuments built in and around the city by Mughal Emperor Aurangzeb.

Flying Down:

Chhatrapati Sambhaji Nagar has a beautiful airport located at the entrance of the city that connects it directly with Delhi, Mumbai, Hyderabad and Bengaluru. By road, the Nagpur-Mumbai expressway passes near the city and is well connected to Mumbai and other major central and western Indian cities. Similar is the case with rail connectivity that enables people to visit Chhatrapati Sambhaji Nagar from all corners of the country.

Moving Around:

Chhatrapati Sambhaji Nagar has a lot to offer in and around the city.

First, let's explore what is within the boundaries of the city. The Bibi ka Maqbara is by far the most outstanding monument in Chhatrapati Sambhaji Nagar. Designed along the lines of the Taj Mahal, it was built by Aurangzeb's son Azam Shah in memory of his mother, Dilras Banu Begum. Often referred to as The Taj of the Deccan, the Maqbara is set amidst a backdrop of hills and with its fountain gardens makes for a definite visit when touring Chhatrapati Sambhaji Nagar.

Near the Bibi Ka Maqbara is the Panchakki – a water mill located inside the Baba Shah Musafir Dargah. The mill was used to grind grains for people visiting the Dargah and is a great example of the scientific manner of architecture that was prevalent even in medieval times.

In the surrounding area of the Maqbara are various monuments and gardens built in the time of Aurangazeb when he had shifted his capital to Daulatabad, a city near Chhatrapati Sambhaji Nagar. One of them is Soneri Mahal, one of the last remaining palaces in the city. It is built against the hills and sports a Rajput style of architecture. Another palace, the Naukhanda Palace, has now become the Aurangabad College for Women.

The Himayat Bagh is a lush green story spread over 400 acres and includes water bodies, a nursery and various species of plants and flowers. The Jama Masjid near Killa Arak can also be visited, where ten pillars are connected by arches to form the structure.

In the city is the Chhatrapati Shivaji Museum which showcases the valour of the Maratha Empire through the centuries. It has on display a 500-year-old armour, an old Paithani saree and even the Holy Quran written by Aurangzeb.

Outside Chhatrapati Sambhaji Nagar, you have three places to visit – Khuldabad, Ajanta and Ellora.

In Khuldabad, which is around 22 km from Chhatrapati Sambhaji Nagar, you can visit the tomb of Aurangzeb; the Dargah of Zar Zari Zar Baksh and Shaikh Burhan ud-din Garib Chishti, as well as the revered Bhadra Maruti Temple where the idol of Lord Hanuman can be seen in a sleeping posture.

Four kilometres ahead of Khuldabad is the UNESCO World Heritage Site of Ellora. A breathtaking lineup of caves that depict Hinduism, Buddhism and Jainism, the array of sculptures, carvings and the sheer scale will leave you awestruck. What will further blow your senses is the famous Kailasa or Kailashnath Temple dedicated to Lord Shiva.

The biggest unique point of the temple is that it has been carved out of one monolithic rock from the Charanandari Hills. Its mammoth size in the shape of a chariot with massive sculptures and carvings is completely mind-boggling. It is an engineering marvel and a case study for history and architecture students.

A kilometre ahead of Ellora is the Grishneshwar Jyotirlinga. Intricately designed with a courtyard around the main temple, Grishneshwar is revered by Hindu devotees from across the country.

On an altogether different route from Chhatrapati Sambhaji Nagar to Jalgaon (around an hour's drive) are the famed Ajanta Caves, another World Heritage Site. These are mostly Buddhist caves in the hills wherein you have to reach there by internal bus from the main gate. From the reception to the first cave is a good climb that prepares you for the awaiting spectacle.

Huge sculptures of Lord Buddha and paintings from the Jataka tales are the highlight of all the 18 caves that one can visit. What is wondrous is that the colour of the paintings is still intact considering that the caves date back to a period between the 2nd century BC and 650 CE.

A note of caution: While travelling from one cave to another, just be very silent and not wave your hands as there are massive bee hives above. Bees get distracted from seeing hand movements and can potentially attack. However, each cave has a security guard manning it, so help is always at hand.

Stay in Comfort:

Apart from being a tourist centre, Chhatrapati Sambhaji Nagar also has many industries around hence the influx of business traveller too is huge. There are many hotels that give you a comfortable stay namely, Ambassador Ajanta, Taj Vivanta, Lemon Tree, and WelcomHotel ITC Rama International. All hotels are close to the airport, hence commuting is not much of an issue.

What to Buy:

Lots. The city boasts of the Himroo weave that was started during the Aurangzeb era. The Himroo weave is found in stoles, sarees, kurtas, fabric and dress material. You can also buy the famous Marathi saree, the Paithani, famous for its bird motifs. Now, the Paithani is also available in ladies suits as well as potli purses. There are many showrooms of Himroo on the highway to Ellora, though a few are in the city as well.

From Ajanta, you can buy rocks of semi-precious stones that are found in the Deccan plateau. There are plenty of shops to be found at the main gate of Ajanta before you board the bus for the caves. You can buy shining and colourful chalcedonites, amethyst, stilbites, chalcedony, etc. Some, you would have never seen before and are in their real form which look exotic. Be prepared to bargain a lot!!

Kanpur

•••

On the Map:

An important financial, military and industrial centre since British colonial rule, Kanpur is located in Central Uttar Pradesh on the banks of the sacred river Ganga. It has also been known as the Manchester of India, owing to the large number of factories, mills, leather tanneries and other industries that used it as home too.

Flying Down:

The newly launched revamped airport of Kanpur now has direct flights to Delhi, Mumbai and Bengaluru. By train, the city is well connected to all parts of the country and the Delhi-Varanasi Vande Bharat has even brought it closer to the National Capital. The Grand

Trunk Road from Amritsar to Kolkata has been passing through Kanpur since colonial times and the road network has further strengthened now.

Moving Around:

If you are on a day's visit to Kanpur, the first place to go to is the Anandeswar Temple, an ancient Shiva Temple that is revered by many. It is situated on the banks of the Ganga and will definitely give you solace.

Other temples in Kanpur that are worth visiting are the JK Temple which is an amalgamation of modern and traditional architecture; the resplendent ISKCON Temple; the Jain Glass Temple, which looks absolutely stunning and the simple yet popular Ram Janki Temple.

Another religious place that you can visit is the beautifully built Kanpur Memorial Church. One of the oldest churches built in India, it is a memoir to the lives lost during the Sepoy Mutiny of 1857.

Kanpur has a number of parks that one can go to in the evening for a stroll. They are the Phool Bagh; the aesthetically designed Gautam Buddha Park replete with sculptures, well-manicured lawns and fountains; the Mahatma Gandhi Park in the Cantonment area and the Nana Rao Park, whose entrance looks like a fortress gate. The Nana Rao Park has sculptures of Tatya Tope, Rani Lakshmi Bai, Lala Lajpat Rai and Ajizan Ba as well as a banyan tree called "Boodha Bargad", symbolising freedom from the English colonisers.

The Moti Jheel is a favourite haunt of locals who go there for a stroll in the evening along the waters partaking in street food from the various food stalls that line up around it.

Another family hangout is the Massacre Ghat. Located on the banks of the Ganga and now called the Nana Rao Ghat, the Ghat is a perfect relaxation point where you can just sit and stare at the river waters beyond. Similar is the case with other Ghats in the city that line up the holy river.

You can also see the Ganga Barrage from the riverfront, an iconic bridge-cum-dam that today defines Kanpur.

Around 24 km from Kanpur lies the idyllic town of Bithoor on the banks of the Ganga. It is an ideal place to find peace and solace in the hustle and bustle of life. It is the birthplace of Rani Laxmi Bai and Saheb Peshwa. The first place to visit in Bithoor is the Valmiki Ashram, where Valmiki wrote the Ramayana.

The Brahmghat is an ideal place to sit and relax in the evening cool breeze from the river. You can also visit the Dhruv Teela, where Dhruv stood on one leg to do penance to Lord Vishnu.

Stay in Comfort:

The three best hotels in Kanpur for a luxurious stay are Hotel Landmark, Regenta Central, The Crystal and Vijay Intercontinental. Rest of the hotels in the city come in the three to two star category.

What to Buy:

Definitely, leather items as the city is home to a lot of tanneries. Apart from this, the most famous sweet of Kanpur made famous by superstar Amitabh Bachchan, Thaggu ke Laddoo. The laddoo is made of khoya and no other sweet shop has the same taste as the one made by Ram Avtar Pandey's chain of sweet shops. He also started the Badnaam Kulfi which has become a rage in the city.

No visit to Kanpur is complete without Thaggu ke Laddoo and Badnaam Kulfi!!

Visakhapatnam

• • •

On the Map:

The port city of Visakhapatnam is located on an embayment in the Bay of Bengal, in the state of Andhra Pradesh and is probably one of the most beautiful cities in India. It is finally getting its due as a major commercial and industrial centre of the region.

Flying Down:

Visakhapatnam has an international airport and has direct flights to Thailand, Malaysia and Singapore. Domestically, it is linked directly to Hyderabad, Chennai, Bengaluru, Mumbai, Delhi and Kolkata. A new Raipur-Visakhapatnam expressway is under construction, making connectivity to the port city even better. The city anyway falls on the Kolkata-Chennai national highway route.

Rail connections too, are at par with the city being well connected to various regions in the country.

Moving Around:

The best place to start your exploration of Visakhapatnam is the RK Beach Road that serves as the marine drive of the country. A drive along the road in the morning makes you come face to face with the blue waters of the Bay of Bengal. In the evening, it turns into a recreational place with locals and tourists alike coming to the road to see the sunset and spend leisure time.

The RK Beach also has a major attraction on its sands in the shape of a submarine. A submarine parked on the beach now serves as a museum, the only one in Asia.

Little ahead of the RK Beach is the famous Rushikonda Beach, aptly known as the Jewel of the East Coast. Its vast expanse of sandy stretches and rocks, approachable by a flight of steps that lead down from a well-manicured garden, exposes a stunning shoreline.

Being a port city, Visakhapatnam has many beaches to boast about. Some others are Ramakrishna Beach, Yarada Beach, Bheemii Beach, Gangavaram Beach and the Lawson's Bay Beach. All of them present a stunning picture of the sun, sea and sand.

Visakhapatnam also has a Victory at Sea Memorial dedicated to those navy personnel who fought during the Indo-Pak war in 1971. It is popular with tourists and instills a feeling of pride and patriotism when you visit.

Further down from Rushikonda Beach atop a hill is located Kailsagiri – a hilltop park that sports a spectacular view of the sea and has two 40 feet statues of Lord Shiva and Goddess Parvati in pure white. The park has a small train that takes you around the area, showcasing various attractions like the Titanic Viewpoint, Floral Spot, Gliding Point, Jungle Trails, Shanti Ashram, Shanku Chakra Nama and many more. A perfect evening out for families!

A few kilometres from Visakhapatnam is the Dolphin's Nose which is a 174 metre headland that gives visitors a view of the lush greenery of the Eastern Ghats.

For children, a visit to the Indira Gandhi Zoo and the Matsyadarshini Aquarium is a perfect recreation for families.

Around 80 km from Visakhapatnam is the "Kashmir of Andhra Pradesh" named Lambasingi, a quaint village nestled in the picturesque Arakku Valley, 1025 m above sea level. It is the only place in South India that witnesses snowfall and offers panoramic views of lush green mountains, valleys shrouded in pale mists and tree-lined pathways that look like paintings rather than reality.

In the hills is located the Kumbalakonda Wildlife Sanctuary that is home to panthers, Sambar deer, spotted deer, barking deer, jackal, wild boar and wild dogs.

Bojjannakonda is a small group of rock-cut caves in the hills that have sculptures of Lord Buddha drawing tourists in large droves on a daily basis.

Stay in Comfort:

Visakhapatnam has many branded hotels like Novotel, The Gateway, Dolphin Hotel, Four Points by Sheraton, WelcomHotel ITC Devee Grand Bay, Radisson Blu, The Park and Fairfield by Marriott. There are many local brands also like Dasapalla, Palm Beach Resort and Dolphin to choose from.

What to Buy:

Since the Araku Valley near Visakhapatnam is famous for its coffee plantations, buying coffee and Araku chocolates is a done thing while in the port city. Apart from this, you can buy Pochampalli silk sarees, brass artefacts, Andhra wooden toys and handicrafts.

Mysuru

On the Map:

Located on the foothills of the Chamundi Hills, Mysuru is in the southern part of Karnataka and has a glorious past that makes it an immensely popular city in India. It is also the gateway to Coorg, one of the most beautiful hill stations in the country. Mysuru is an important tourist destination and its proximity to Bengaluru makes it easily accessible.

Flying Down:

Mysuru airport is small and hence it is only directly connected with Chennai and Hyderabad as of now. The new Bengaluru-Mysuru expressway makes it possible to reach the city in just over three hours. Vande Bharat too, connects it with Bengaluru and Chennai.

Moving Around:

The first place on your visit list in Mysuru has to be the Mysuru Palace. It is simply exquisite. A former palace of the royal family of Mysuru – the Wodeyars – the Mysuru Palace is one of the biggest palaces in the country. Built with the Chamundi Hills in the background, the Palace is famous for its intricate carvings, sculptures and the Indo-Saracenic style of architecture. The façade itself will leave you in awe as you walk through the gates towards the counter for tickets.

I had hired the services of a government-accredited guide from the entrance who took me around effortlessly, explaining everything in detail.

Inside you will be mesmerised by the Durbar Hall with its ornate ceiling and sculpted pillars and the Kalyanmantapa with its glazed tile flooring, domed ceiling and stained glass. There is a sound and light show too in the evening, telling you more about the history of the palace.

The Palace hosts the famous Mysuru Dasara which is a tradition that has been followed for more than 400 years, wherein a beautiful procession is taken out by the royal family on elephants, commemorating the triumph of good over evil.

You can also visit the Jagmohan Palace where the royal family lived before the Mysore Palace was built. The Jagmohan Palace houses a number of paintings and is regarded as one of the oldest buildings in the city.

Mysuru

The next go-to place in Mysuru is the famous Brindavan Gardens. Built across the Kaveri River, the gardens were built by the then Maharaja Krishnaraja Wodeyar on the lines of the Shalimar Gardens in Kashmir. Spread over 60 acres with lawns and fountains, the beauty of the Brindavan Gardens is best seen in the evening when it is lit up. The Freedom Fighter's Park within the city is also known for its well-manicured lawns, flower varieties and nicely designed pathways and sitting areas.

Near the Palace is the Shaku Vana that has over 200 species of birds and a visit to the famous Sri Chamarajendra Zoological Gardens is a perfect day out for families with kids. There is also the Bonsai Garden which has over 100 different varieties spread over four acres. A favourite picnic spot for locals, the Karanji Lake, also has hundreds of species of birds visiting its shores, which will be a cherry on the top for bird watchers. Similar is the case with Lingambudhi Lake.

After Delhi, Mysuru is the only city in India that has a Rail Museum, depicting the journey and developments of the Indian Railways.

The Chamundeshwari Temple located atop a hill that gives you panoramic views of Mysuru is a must-visit. Dating back to the 12th century, the Goddess Chamundeswari is the kuldevi of the royal family of Mysuru. The deity idol is in gold and the gopuram looks ethereal in yellow and white. You can also visit the ancient Trineswaraswamy Temple near the palace dedicated to Lord Shiva for obeisance.

St. Philomena's Church with its tall spires is another tourist attraction that you can visit in Mysuru.

Some places you can visit outside the city are Krishnarajsagar Dam, the Balmuri Waterfalls, Edmuri Waterfalls and the temple town of Nanjangud also known as Southern Kashi, where the main temple is dedicated to Lord Shiva.

Stay in Comfort:

Being a popular tourist city, Mysuru has many brands that have opened their properties here, namely Radisson Blu, Grand Mercure, Fortune JP Palace, Southern Star, Windflower Resorts and Spa among others in three star and two-star categories.

What to Buy:

Mysuru is literally a shopaholic's paradise. The city is known for its silk sarees, incense, sandalwood products and coffee from the nearby regions of Coorg. Mysuru silk is extremely famous and you can buy sarees, fabric, and suit material of the same. The city has always been synonymous with sandalwood and you can buy artefacts, soaps, perfumes and incense made of the same.

Siliguri

• • •

On the Map:

Located at the foothills of the Darjeeling Hills in Northern Bengal, Siliguri is the largest city in this part of the country. It is flanked by the Mahananda and Teesta Rivers and is the gateway to the Northeast, making it a major transportation and trading hub of the region. It has been known for the four T's: Tourism, Timber, Tea and Transport.

Flying Down:

Tourists going to Darjeeling, Kalimpong and Sikkim usually take flights to the Bagdogra airport, 16 km from Siliguri. There are direct flights to Kolkata, Guwahati, Delhi, Mumbai, Chennai, Hyderabad and Bengaluru. A new expressway from Varanasi to Siliguri is under construction which will further enhance road connectivity with the city. All trains going to the North-East, stop at the New Jalpaiguri Station that is near Siliguri.

Moving Around:

Siliguri is known for its beautiful natural surroundings, tea gardens, temples and monasteries. When visiting, the first place to start your tour should be the Salugara Monastery. The monastery looks splendid with its white stupa, offset by the colourful flags. The 100 feet stupa was founded by Tibetan Lama, Kalu Rinpoche.

Next is the ISKCON Temple, known as the Sri Sri Radha Madhav Sundar Mandir, with its grand structure, peaceful ambience and spiritual feel. Near the city centre is the Lokenath Temple that is dedicated to Lord Shiva, which also has idols of Goddess Parvati and Lord Ganesha.

For families with kids, a visit to the North Bengal Science City with its planetarium and Nature Interpretation Centre is a must, for an enjoyable and a learning experience.

The best place to witness nature up, close and personal is the Coronation Bridge which is located in Darjeeling district, some 23 km from Siliguri. It is built over the Teesta River, with lush green mountains as its backdrop and makes for a perfect morning outing in pleasant weather. Close to the Coronation Bridge is the ancient Sevoke Kali Mandir which is situated on the banks of the Teesta River and is revered by locals.

On the outskirts of Siliguri is the Madhuban Park, built by the Indian Army, a restful place in lush green surroundings and a favourite picnic sport for people in the city.

A visit to Siliguri is incomplete without a walk in a tea garden, most of which are located outside the city. There are a number of tea estates that take you on a tour of the sloping plantation (that makes for awesome instagrammable photographs) as well as enable you to taste some of their different varieties of tea.

If you have a day to spare, you can visit Dudhia, a quaint little town on the meandering Balason River that makes for an idyllic romantic setting. Or take a safari in the Mahananda Wildlife Sanctuary that is home to deer, tigers, elephants, migratory birds and bison.

Stay in Comfort:

Siliguri has a mix of business, leisure and tea garden hotels you will not find anywhere else. Some brands are LemonTree, Courtyard by Marriott, Cygnett, Ramada Encore and the Mayfair Tea Estate.

What to Buy:

Tea and wooden artefacts since the area is known for timber. Some of the markets that are popular in the city are Hong Kong Market, Hill Carter Road and Sevoke Road.

Rajkot and Junagadh

•••

On the Map:

Rajkot and Junagadh are located in the Kathiawar Peninsula in the Saurashtra region of Gujarat. Rajkot is the biggest city in Saurashtra and currently the only one with a functional airport. It is one of the most prominent industrial and commercial centres in the country. Junagadh is a little more than 100 km from Rajkot and is famous for its forts, palaces and cave temples. It is located at the foothills of the Girnar hills and is the gateway to the famous Gir National Park as well as the Somnath Jyotirlinga.

Flying Down:

Rajkot has an international airport that caters to the entire Saurashtra region. While international flights are yet to start, domestically

Rajkot, is connected with daily flights to Delhi, Mumbai, Bengaluru and Goa. Since the airport is new, it is expected that flights to other destinations will begin soon. Highway connecting Ahmedabad to Rajkot is comparable to any outside the country, while rail connectivity too, is at par with major metros, considering the importance of Rajkot. The Rajkot Junagadh highway is smooth, though Junagadh can also be approached via Ahmedabad through a different route.

Moving Around:

Having been a princely state, Rajkot has the Ranjit Vilas Palace that gives you a glimpse into the lifestyle of the erstwhile royal family. However, you can see the Palace from the outside as it is not open to the public and is the private residence of the royal descendants. It has been designed in Mughal, Gothic and Victorian architecture.

The Swaminarayan Mandir and the Jagat Mandir are two must-visit temples in the city. While the former is known for its opulent and intricate architecture, the latter is made of red sandstone with the chief deity being Shri Ramakrishna Paramhansa.

Rajkot is also the city where Mahatma Gandhi spent his early years. You can visit the Kaba Gandhi no Delo, which is the house where Gandhiji lived when his father was the Diwan of Rajkot. The house is now a museum showcasing aspects of Gandhiji's early life.

To learn about the history of the Jadeja Dynasty that founded Rajkot, you can visit the Watson Museum which showcases many artefacts related to the royal clan and give you a glimpse into their lifestyle. Jubilee Garden in the city centre is a large green space that also houses a museum, a children's play area, an auditorium and the Lang Library.

44 km from Rajkot is the Tankara Museum which showcases the historical importance of Rajkot and is the birthplace of Swami Dayanand, the founder of Arya Samaj. The Museum also tells you more about his values, beliefs and teachings.

There are two dams outside of Rajkot – the Nyari Dam and the Aji Dam. These are favourite picnic spots for locals. On the outskirts of the city is the Lalpari Lake, the favourite haunt of those looking to spot migratory birds.

35 km away is the quaint town of Gondal, famous for its touch of royalty, evident through the Riverside Palace which now serves as a heritage hotel and Darbargadh Palace. Near Gondal are the Khambhalida Caves, that are a set of three caves dedicated to Lord Buddha and his teachings. Further down is Analgadh, famous for its valley views, lush greenery and water bodies.

A two-hour drive will bring you into historical Junagadh that is home to a number of forts, palaces and monuments. You can start your tour of the city by visiting over 2,000-year-old Uparkot Fort. Built during the Mauryan Empire, the Fort down the ages has seen many occupations and today its complex houses Buddhist caves, mosques, tombs, step wells and temples. There is also a square-shaped lake and a moat around the Fort that used to have crocodiles to ward off enemies.

The Mausoleum of Bahuddanbhai Hussainbhai is a unique architectural monument that stands apart in Junagadh. The Mahabat Maqbara as it is called, has four minarets with winding staircases, elaborate stone carvings and intricate arches. The Jama Masjid too is located nearby. You can also visit the Darbar Hall Museum which showcases the Nawabi lifestyle of the 19th century rulers of Junagadh.

One of the main attractions of Junagadh is Girnar Hill which finds mention even in the Vedas and the Mohen-jo-daro period. Visited by Hindus and Jains as there are temples dedicated to both religions in the Hills, the path upwards to Girnar Hill is an adventure in itself, giving viewers a breathtaking view of the Gir National Park around. En route to the Girnar Hill, you will also encounter the 14 edicts of Emperor Asoka.

The Gir National Park is the sole home of the Asiatic Lion and is a must-go to see the King of the Jungle.

At the foothills of the Girnar range is the Damodar Kund water reserve which is revered by Hindus and has a temple and ghats that also serve as a cremation place. Also at the foothills is the Wellingdon Dam, a favourite tourist place for the locals.

Stay in Comfort:

Rajkot has some prime hotels for a luxurious stay like The Fern, The Imperial, Sarovar Portico, Lemon Tree, Sayyaji, Platinum and the Khirasara Palace Heritage Hotel.

What to Buy:

Rajkot is famous for a saree by the same name, known for its patola weaves in different colours. A visit to the city is incomplete without buying namkeen and the mirch chutney from the famous Rasikbhai Chevdavala, where you can buy the famous potato jaali wafers of Rajkot, thepla, different varieties of chevda, gathiya, sev, bakharwadi, sing, chakari, bhakhari, etc.

Indore

On the Map:
The commercial capital of Madhya Pradesh, Indore has a rich history and is known for its street food, handloom industry, temples and retail centres. Indore is today continuously been ranked as the cleanest city in India. When you visit Indore, you will find it completely spic and span. The city is also the education hub in the state, with both IIM and IIT having campuses here.

Flying Down:
Indore has direct flights to Delhi, Mumbai, Hyderabad, Bengaluru, Chennai, Kolkata, Ahmedabad, Surat, Jaipur, Udaipur, Lucknow, Pune, Chandigarh and Goa. This big lineup shows the importance

of the city. Road connectivity is at par with metros and the Mumbai highway is a dream to drive on. Same is the case with rail connectivity, which is seamless and connects the city with all corners of the country.

Moving Around:

Having been the seat of the Holkar Dynasty, Indore is home to many palaces and forts dating back to the medieval period. The foremost among them are the Rajwada and Lal Bagh Palace.

The Rajwada will mesmerise you with its 200-year-old grand building with well laid-out gardens with fountains. Its opulent interiors will take your breath away and a scintillating sound and light show takes place on select days that will tell you more about the history and mystery of the royal palace.

The other royal property, the Lal Bagh Palace is 3 km from the city and showcases the rich lifestyle of the Holkar rulers, replete with artefacts from India and abroad like Persian carpets, stained glass from Belgium, stuffed animal heads, grand chandeliers, marble flooring and pillars, paintings, etc.

Gandhi Hall looks stunning in white marble and red sandstone, designed in the Indo-Gothic style and named after the Father of the Nation. The White Church will remind us of similar churches in Goa.

Indore is home to a few green spaces that make for an afternoon visit in the shade like the Nehru Park, the Kamla Nehru Prani Sangrahlaya, Pipliyapala Regional Park, the Meghdoot Garden or the Chhatri Bagh which was the official burial place of the Holkar royals. Alternatively, if you are a history buff, you can visit various museums in the city like the Royal Museum, Kanha Museum and the Indore Museum.

Some of the famous temples in Indore that are worth visiting are the Geeta Bhawan, Bijasen Tekri perched atop a hill, the Bada Ganpati Temple, ISKCON Indore, the Kanch Jain Mandir, Gommat Giri Jain Temples, the popular Annapoorna Temple and the Khajrana Ganesh Temple.

Around Indore are located a few waterfalls that make for a perfect picnic like the Patalpani Waterfalls, Tincha Falls, Mohadi Falls, Bamniya Kund, Hathyari Khoh and the Chidiya and Jog Bhadak Waterfalls. Just 10 km away is the Ralamandal Wildlife Sanctuary, home to various flora and fauna nestled alongside the Narmada River.

However, if you have a day to spare, you must visit Maheshwar, a quaint little town on the banks of the Narmada that has a famous fort-cum-palace of the same name with its own Ghats on the river that are an absolute delight to see. The Ghats have been a setting for many historical movies and are still well preserved.

While walking down to the Palace and the ghats through the winding streets of the small town, you will come across many stores selling Maheshwari weave sarees, dress materials and dupattas. Worth a Buy!

Stay in Comfort:

Some of the bigger hotels in Indore are Radisson Blu, Sayyaji, Fairfield by Marriott, Lemon Tree, Sarovar Portico, Ramada Encore by Wyndham, Eseentia Luxury Hotel, Celebrations, etc. There are several three-star budget hotels that are quite good for a comfortable stay like Best Western, Amar Vilas and many more.

What to Buy:

Arguably, as mentioned earlier, the Maheshwari weave sarees, suit material, dupatta or men's kurtas. But a visit to Indore is incomplete without a trip to the Sarafa Market for jewellery or to partake street at the Chappan Street where there are 56 outlets serving sumptuous Indian snacks. In fact, the Sarafa Market as well as the road outside Marriott too comes alive at night, with numerous street food stalls that are a foodie's delight.

Varanasi

• • •

On the Map:

Considered as one of the oldest living cities in the world, Varanasi (or Banaras or Kashi as it's also known) is the cosmos of Hinduism where you can see the circle of life and death, all at the banks of the Holy Ganga. It is located in Eastern Uttar Pradesh and is home to the most revered Kashi Vishwanath Jyotirlinga and is believed to be the city where you attain Moksha. Mark Twain once said, **'The Indian city of Varanasi was 'older than history, older than tradition, older even than legend'.**

Flying Down:

Being an important spiritual and pilgrim centre, Varanasi is well connected by air, rail and road to all parts of India. It has direct flights to Delhi, Mumbai, Kolkata, Chennai, Hyderabad, Bengaluru and many other Tier 2 cities across the country. The Delhi-Varanasi Vande Bharat Express connects it to the Capital and other parts of India. It has superfast trains linking it to other cities also. Highways around Varanasi connect it well to other states.

Moving Around:

For long, the lanes and by-lanes of Varanasi coupled with the Ghats on the Ganga, have attracted pilgrims and tourists by the hordes. However, after the revamp of the Kashi Vishwanath Corridor, the number of tourists to the ancient city has quadrupled and today it surpasses Goa.

Your first stop in Varanasi has to be the Kashi Vishwanath Temple. It is one of the 12 Jyotirlingas and is located on the banks of the Ganga. After the construction of its corridor, now it looks completely different, more spacious, breathable and pious. It has not only preserved its heritage but now looks as grand as it used to look in ancient times.

The Temple now has its own ghat adjoining the other major ghats like Dashashwamedh, Assi, Manikarnika, etc. It is the evening Ganga Aarti at Dashashwamedh that is truly mesmerising and a spectacle to watch. You can see the Aarti either by sitting on the steps at Dashashwamedh Ghat or from a boat opposite the Ghat on the river. The Aarti mostly lasts half an hour and is an experience that one must undertake.

There are various types of boats available at the ghats – motorboats, the original rowing ones or bigger cruise ships. One can take an open boat to witness the five-kilometre long ghats. You should take one boat trip in the evening just before the Aarti and another in early morning from 6:00 am to 8:00 am before the sun rises above your head, to witness the historical and spiritual splendour of the ghats in the cool morning breeze.

You can go in the maze of lanes and by-lanes behind the Ghat towards the Gowdolia Chowk, which too now wears a new look. You can spend time shopping, having street food, for which Varanasi is famous. In one of the by-lanes near the Kashi Vishwanath Temple is the Kaal Bhairav Temple which is visited by thousands of devotees.

Other temples that one must visit are the Durga Temple which looks beautiful with its red colour offset by the shimmering waters of the small lake next to it; the Shri Satyanarayan Tulsi Manas Mandir named after Saint Tulsidas; Sankat Mochan Hanuman Temple and the Bharat Mata Temple.

Opposite the Tulsi Ghat is the Ramnagar Fort that is home to the royal family of Varanasi. It was built in 1750 as per Mughal style or architecture. You can also go on a drive inside the Banaras Hindu University (BHU), one of the most prestigious universities in the country, spread over 1300 acres. BHU also has its own Kashi Vishwanath Temple, designed on the lines of the original one and a drive in the campus will give you a feel of its expanse.

Some 10 km away from Varanasi is Sarnath, the place where Lord Buddha started his journey of Dharma. Here, you can visit the Dhamek Stupa as part of the Sarnath Archaelogical Site from where Lord Buddha revealed his eightfold path; the Chaukhandi Stupa, where Lord Buddha first met his disciples; the Mahabodhi Society Temple, built in the Gupta period; The Thai Temple, Tibetan Temple and Temples built by various Buddhist majority countries in their architectural style like that from Sri Lanka, Japan, China, Myanmar, etc.

You can also have dinner at one of the heritage hotels located on the ghats like the Guleria Kothi or the BrijRama, to get a feel of history.

Stay in Comfort:

There is no dearth of options in Varanasi in all budgets. Some of the four and five star properties are BrijRama; Guleria Kothi; Radisson; India Benares; HHI Varanasi; Rivatas by ideal; The Fern Residency; Taj Ganges; Double Tree by Hilton; Clarks and more.

What to Buy:

Without doubt, the Banarasi Silk Saree, suit or fabric, a weave that has been famous from time immemorial. There are numerous shops selling this around the Ghat area or near the Station.

No trip to Varanasi is complete if you do not partake in sumptuous street food like chat, blue lassi, kachori, bhel, paan, etc.

Jewellery, bangles and puja related products are other items you can think of buying too.

Kannur

•••

On the Map:

An important city in North Kerala also known as Malabar, Kannur abounds in beaches and is also the gateway to the picturesque hill station of Wayanad. The lush green surroundings overlooking the Arabian Sea makes for a picture-perfect location for a quick getaway.

Flying Down:

Kannur has a big revamped airport but has very few flights as of now. It is directly connected to Kochi, Bengaluru, Chennai, Hyderabad and Mumbai. Vande Bharat which connects the length of Kerala, stops at Kannur as well connecting it easily to all parts of the state. By road, Kannur is accessible via Coimbatore too apart from the Mumbai-Thiruvananthapuram highway.

Moving Around:

Since Kannur has a number of beautiful beaches, you can start exploring the city from its shoreline. On the shore road above the beach, you can stop at a vantage point to get a glimpse of the Baby Beach. A small beach area with a flight of steps going down to its smooth sandy stretch, Baby Beach is a perfect picnic spot for those who are looking for less crowded beaches.

However, the main beach in Kannur that is synonymous with the city is the Payyambalam Beach. A long stretch of golden sands, it is one of the most beautiful beaches in Kerala and makes for a perfect sunset point for anyone visiting Kannur. A few kilometres ahead and an extension of the Payyambalam Beach is the Meenkannu Beach which is unspoilt and serene. You can even see the Kannur Lighthouse from the beach that looks romantic in the night when lit up.

Between Kannur and Thalassery is located the Thottada Beach, known for its palm trees and sandy stretch. Another palm fringed beach is the Ezhara Beach, some 8 km away from Kannur. 15 km away is the Dharmadam Beach which is located on an island that you can wade through from the shoreline during low tide.

However, what takes the cake in Kannur in terms of beaches is the longest drive-in beach in India, the Muzhapillangad. Around 12 km from Kannur, Muzhapillangad is a stunning 4 km sandy road that offers you the luxury to drive and see the captivating view of the sea, especially during sunset from the confines of your car. I saw many families enjoying a picnic on the beach with their cars parked right next to where they were sitting. Lots of others were racing on the beach in their cars or bikes, since the expanse of the beach is huge.

The St Angelo Fort is one of the most popular tourist attractions in Kannur after the sandy stretches. It overlooks the Mopila Bay and was built by the first Viceroy of Portugal to India in the 1500s. It commands majestic views of the sea and exudes a historical charm that has many stories to tell.

Bringing life to mystical legends is the Theyyam dance form. It is one of the most riveting art forms of Malabar, made popular across India by the Kannada blockbuster, Kantara. These dance performances takes place often in temples, between October and May every year with the most popular months being November and December. You can plan your visit to Kannur accordingly if you want to see the Theyyam dance.

The Muthappan Temple in Parassinakadavu, 16 km from Kannur, witnesses the Theyyam dance practically every day. The town is also home to a snake park, one of its kind in Kerala.

You can also visit the Peralssery Subrahmanya Temple where it is believed that Lord Ram and Lord Lakshmana visited and left a bangle (Peruvala) on their way to Lanka to free Goddess Sita.

Madayipara, the land of flowers, is 21 km from Kannur. Nestled in the Western Ghats, it is popular for its landscape and considered to be one of the most beautiful in the state.

Stay in Comfort:

Bang on the Payyambalam Beach is the Krishna Beach Resort, the most popular luxury property in Kannur. However, I stayed in a new property called the State Beach Resort that had simply the most stunning view I have ever seen. It is perched atop a cliff and all its rooms, especially those on the first floor look out onto the sea, providing you with views to kill for. I would not recommend any city hotels as staying inside a beach city like Kannur is a complete waste of time and money.

What to Buy:

Theyyam masks. Since this is Theyyam country, you must buy the Theyyam mask or other souvenirs linked to it. Other items to buy are handicrafts, sarees, earthenware and jewellery.

Madurai

On the Map:
With a history that goes back 2500 years, Madurai is the second largest city in Tamil Nadu located on the River Vaigai and is famous for the Sri Meenakshi Amman Temple and the Jasmine Flower. The city is built around the temple, which is its fulcrum and a major religious tourism centre in the state.

Flying Down:
The city has an international airport with flights to South East Asia and Sri Lanka. Apart from international, domestically Madurai is directly connected to Chennai, Bengaluru, Hyderabad, Mumbai and Delhi. The highway to Chennai and Coimbatore is a smooth ride and so is rail connectivity to other parts of the state and the country.

Moving Around:

A visit to Madurai has to start with the Meenakshi Sundareswarar Temple, which is dedicated to Goddess Parvati and her consort Sundareswara, a form of Lord Shiva. Built during the Pandyan Empire starting in 1190 AD and restored during the Vijayanagar Empire in the 16th century, the Meenakshi Temple is spread over 14 acres and has 14 gopurams, numerous sculpted pillars, intricately designed walls and ceilings, a water reservoir, innumerable shrines and mandapams.

The Temple has four gates named after the four directions – East, West, South and North. Each entrance has closets to keep your footwear, deposit mobiles and buy items for puja inside. The gopurams on the four gates can be seen from afar and are connected to each other by an outer boundary wall. The temple is surrounded by markets on all sides, selling anything from handicrafts to puja items to utensils, etc.

The Temple complex also houses administrative offices, elephant enclosures and residences. As you enter through the gate, you will be awestruck at the scale of the temple – its intricate carvings, sculptures of various Gods and Goddesses adorning walls, ceilings, pillars and more.

The other temple you must visit in Madurai is the Alagar Koil. It is dedicated to Lord Vishnu. 5 km from the Meenakshi Temple is the Mariamman Teppakulam, which has been constructed in honour of Lord Vigneswara. The temple has a huge pond in its compound, giving it a magnificent feel. Other temples of note are the Pazhamudhir Solai, dedicated to Lord Subrahmanya and the Tirupparankundram Murugan Temple, dedicated to Mother Earth and is a masterpiece of architecture.

Apart from these Temples, you should visit the Thirumalai Nayakar Mahal. Built in the 17th century by the then King (Nayak) of Madurai by the same name, the palace is a perfect blend of Dravidian and Rajput styles of architecture.

Excursions outside the city include the Samanar Hills 8 km from Madurai which are home to Jain caves and the Kutladampatti Falls which is 30 km away and makes for an ideal picnic spot for locals.

Stay in Comfort:

Some luxury properties in Madurai include Courtyard by Marriott, JC Residency, Fortune Pandiyan Hotel, Regency by GRT, The Gateway, Astoria and Poppy's. Other 3-star and budget-category hotels also provide options to those looking for something cheaper.

What to Buy:

Madurai is famous for Madurai Silk Sarees, handicrafts, brassware, wooden carvings, jewellery and puja items. Jasmine is famous too, though it won't be possible to bring it with you as it will wither away after a day. On your visit to Madurai, you must have the famous Jigarthanda, a refreshing drink that is unique to the city. It is made of milk, rose syrup, almonds, ice cream and sugar.

Bhuj

• • •

On the Map:

The main city of Kutch, Bhuj is located between the sandy, marshy Kutch and the Gulf of Kutch. The city is full of palaces, temples and forts and is the gateway to the Rann of Kutch as well as the Rann Utsav tent city. Its traditional handicrafts, the lippan work and embroidery with beads and mirrors are world-famous and make the city a shopper's paradise.

Flying Down:

Since it's a small place, Bhuj does not have many flight options. The only direct flight it has is to Ahmedabad and Mumbai. The highways in Gujarat are to die for. They are excellent and even the roads to villages around Bhuj are well maintained. Rail network connects the city directly with other parts of Gujarat as well as North and Western India.

Moving Around:

The first place on your tour list has to be the White Desert of Kutch. The world's largest salt desert, the place is an hour from Bhuj and is ideal to visit in the evening to see the sunset. However, since the whole place is marshy, it is recommended not to go deep inside the desert because of quicksand. The trip to the White Desert should also include Kala Doongar and India Bridge.

Kala Doongar is the highest point of Kutch and it is from here that you can see the White Desert in all its entirety. A bridge called the India Bridge needs to be crossed to get into the White Desert. It also has the BSF outpost and will give you a patriotic feeling when you reach there.

Within the city, the first place to see is the Aaina Mahal. Built during the 18th century by the Ruler of Kutch, the palace today has a museum of handicrafts where all the crafts from Kutch are showcased. Next to the Aaina Mahal is the Prag Mahal, which is open for visitors and shows you the lifestyle of the Bhuj royal family and its intricate architecture of the building.

A prominent feature of the Prag Mahal is the Clock Tower, which has been featured in many Gujarati and Bollywood movies.

The Hamirsar Lake in the middle of the city, is a perfect evening out for locals when its cool breeze gives you relief from the afternoon scorching sun. In the winter, you can also see migratory birds flocking to its shores.

Another place to visit is the exquisitely built Swaminarayan Temple. Built way back in 1882, the Temple is one of the first Swaminarayan Temples to be built and sports the same intricately designed arches, pillars, domes and mandaps.

To see an aerial view of the city and the hills around, you can climb 200 steps up the Bhujia Hill outside the city. However, right on the hill is one new tourist attraction that you should not miss. That is the Smritivan Earthquake Memorial Museum. Probably the biggest such museum to be built in India, it is spread over 470 acres and is in memory of the victims of the devastating earthquake of 2001.

The Memorial has 50 check-dam reservoirs that house the nameplates of almost 13,000 victims of the 2001 earthquake. It also consists of the world's largest Miyawaki Forest with over 3 lakh plants, spread across the entire memorial to create a living, breathing monument that also serves as the lungs for the city of Bhuj.

An hour from Bhuj is the famous Mandvi Beach, located on the grounds of the beautiful Vijay Vilas Palace that was made famous by the movie Hum Dil De Chuke Sanam where it was shot. The beach is secluded and no large crowds can be seen there. Camel rides on the beach are a fun way for kids to enjoy.

Stay in Comfort:

Accommodation in Bhuj is a combination of city hotels and resorts near the Rann of Kutch. In the resort category, by far the best is the Rann Utsav by Gujarat Tourism which is simply the most unique experience you will ever have. Others are Kutch Safari Lodge and Regenta Resort which also offer a comfortable stay. Amongst the city hotels, the good ones are Click Hotel, Hotel Prince Residency, Comfort Inn Prince and The Fern Residency.

What to Buy:

We bought so much that we had to pay extra for baggage check-in at the airline counter. You can buy AC quilts, embroidered gaghra choli with mirror work, mirror and bead work blouses, men's kurtas, western dresses, etc.

Udupi

∴

On the Map:

Just less than an hour away from the commercial and industrial hub of Mangaluru, Udupi in Karnataka, is a coastal town that is famous for its cuisine, the Krishna Mutt and beautiful serene beaches. Udupi is part of the Tulunadu region, which extends from Udupi to North Kerala's Kasaragod. The language spoken in Udupi is Tulu apart from Kannada. Manipal, which is famous for its educational institutes, is an extension of Udupi.

Flying Down:

The nearest airport to Udupi is Manguluru, which has direct flights to Bengaluru, Chennai, Hyderabad, Mumbai and Delhi apart from some services to the Gulf. The highway from Mumbai to Kochi passes via Udupi and the railway too is connected to most parts of the country and the state.

Moving Around:

The Udupi Sri Krishna Matha, as the Krishna Temple is known as, is one of the most famous pilgrim centres in South India. Here, Janmasthami is a sight to behold. Built over a 1,000 years ago, the Temple is surrounded by a small pond; the deity in gold and precious jewels can be seen through a window with nine holes called the Navagraha Kitiki. Men need to be bare chested to visit the temple as per ritual and whole complex with life size sculptures at the entrance, will transport you into the realm of spirituality.

The Krishna Matha complex is adorned with beautiful buildings, temples and shops selling puja items. One temple you can visit as it is located right next to the Matha, is the Chandramouleshwara Temple, dedicated to Lord Shiva. The Temple is believed to be older than the Krishna Matha.

The Anantheswara Temple is located right inside the Matha and is believed to be the oldest in the region. It is also dedicated to Lord Shiva with the main shrine being made in stone. Renowned philosopher Madhavacharya used to teach his disciples in this temple.

Apart from visits to temples, the next big attraction of Udupi is its beaches. On top of the list is Malpe. Just 6 km from Udupi city centre, Malpe is the most popular beach in the area and its white sandy stretch is home to many shacks and water sports activities. When I visited the beach, it was packed with tourists and I was told it attracts people from far and wide. A major attraction at Malpe is the Sea Walk. A stretch of concrete walkaway built in the middle of the sea for about 450 metres, the Sea Walk makes for great instagrammable pictures.

From Malpe, you even have excursions going upto St Mary's Island, which is 4 km from the coast. A group of four islands, St Mary's is full of sandy beaches, marine life, crystalline rocks and is a 3-4 hour trip from the mainland.

Towards the direction leading to Manguluru, falls the Kaup or Kapu Beach, popular for its lighthouse, set sand and a number of cheaper accommodations nearby making it a backpacker's paradise.

One beach that you must visit is Delta Beach. More than 30 km from Udupi, the beach (also known as Kodi Bengare Beach) is simply spectacular and nothing like what you would have seen before. As the name suggests, it is a beach on the delta of Suvarna River, where it flows into the Arabian Sea. The beach is an elongated sandy stretch that has sea on three sides, making it a unique experience. When you reach the corner of the delta with the river on one side and the sea on the other – it's a feeling that can't be put into words.

In Kodi Bengare is also located the Hoode Beach. You can also visit Mattu Beach which is 8 km from Udupi. En route to Delta Beach is the Kemmannu Hanging Bridge over the Suvarna River that is also now used for adventure sports.

If you have a day to spare, some 58 km from Udupi is the famous Maravanthe Beach whose aerial pictures are viral on social media. The beach has the sea on one side and the Souparnika River on the other, making it a unique proposition for tourists.

An extension of Udupi (and one never knows when the boundaries blur) is Manipal, the by now famous educational hub of medical, engineering and other institutes. You can take a drive around the town to get a feel of the place. Manipal and the road in Udupi that leads up to it has students all over and modern cafes that mirror Mumbai or Bengaluru catering to the Gen Z.

Stay in Comfort:

Some luxury hotels that you can stay at in Udupi-Manipal are Country Inn and Suites by Radisson, Tea Tree Suites, Hotel Central Park and Paradise Isle Beach Resort. There are a few resorts that are located on the river or near the beach outside the city.

What to Buy:

Wooden and brass artefacts, idols of deities, puja items, incense, etc. There are a number of shops all around the Sri Krishna Matha and it is the ideal place to buy these souvenirs. Consider buying idols of the Udupi Krishna in black marble dust, which is different from what is there in North India and would be a good item for gifting.

Warangal

•••

On the Map:

The second largest city in Telangana, Warangal served as the capital of the illustrious Kakatiya Dynasty, which started its reign in 1163. The Kakatiya imprint can be found all over the city in the form of forts, palaces, temples, lakes, monuments, et al.. A heritage city, Warangal is also called Oru Kallu locally, which means 'a single stone' as people believe that the city was carved out of a single rock in medieval times.

Flying Down:

Since Warangal is 110 kms away from Hyderabad, the airport in Telangana's capital only serves Warangal; Hyderabad is more than well connected with all major cities in India and abroad. The highway from Hyderabad to Warangal is like a carpet on the road and makes for an imminently smooth ride. The rail connection too is well-networked.

Moving Around:

A city that exudes history is the best way to describe Warangal. A tour of the city should start with its most famous landmark – the Thousand Pillars Temple. As the name itself suggests, the temple has a thousand intricately carved pillars dedicated to three deities – Lord Vishnu, Lord Shiva and Lord Surya. It is an ancient pilgrim centre designed in true Kakatiya and Chalukyan style and its architecture is in the shape of a star. The temple attracts thousands of devotees on a daily basis and is the most revered place in the region.

Another landmark of the city is the Warangal Fort. The Fort is a perfect example of architectural marvel and history. Exuding medieval charm, it is spread over 19 km and was constructed in the 13th century by the Kakatiya King, Ganpati Deva. It is very famous for its intricately carved walls, pillars and arches.

Close to the Fort is the Kakatiya Rock Garden which has sculptures of animals like deer, lion, sambar, antelope, etc.

The third ancient architectural attraction in Warangal is the famous Bhadrakali Temple. Dating back to 625 AD of the Chalukyan era, the Temple is located at the edge of a lake and gives pilgrims an amazing experience of sitting and relaxing in its courtyard, after paying respects to Goddess Kali, the deity of the temple. One unique aspect of the deity is that unlike idols in similar temples across the country, the idol here is adorned with weapons in all eight arms and the statue is in a sitting posture with a crown on its head.

Other temples one can visit in Warangal are the ISKCON Temple; the Veernarayana Temple which was built in 1104 AD and dedicated to a form of Lord Vishnu; Inavolu Mallana Temple of Mallikarjun Swamy, an incarnation of Lord Shiva; the ancient Rayaparthy Shiva Temple and the Padmakshi Temple.

Around Warangal are water bodies that make for perfect picnic spots or evening outs. One is the Pakhal Lake, 50 km from the city. Set amidst lush greenery, this man-made lake borders a wildlife sanctuary. Another is the Laknavaram Lake at a similar distance from the city. It has three islands connected by a hanging bridge.

Govindarajalu Gutta is a hill surrounded by forests that are a nature lover's delight. The Hill gives a spectacular view of the city that is unparalleled. A small temple dedicated to Lord Rama is built atop the hill.

Stay in Comfort:

Warangal does not have any major hospitality brands setting shop but it does have local players. Some of the hotels that you can choose from are - Hotel Thousand Pillars, Venketeswara Mitra Residency, Hotel ML Grand, Hotel Shreya, Suprabha Hotel and Landmark Hotel.

What to Buy:

Warangal is famous for its handicrafts, handlooms, and traditional crafts. You can visit the Lepakshi Handicrafts Emporium, Subedari, DWCRA Bazaar and Hanumakonda for Brassware, Khadi items, dhurries and scroll paintings. The Pochampalli saree is also a good option to buy when visiting the city.

Chandigarh

•••

On the Map:

A Union Territory located on the foothills of the Shivalik range, serving as the Capital of the two states that flank it, Punjab and Haryana, Chandigarh is also known as 'City Beautiful'. Designed by French architect Le Corbusier, Chandigarh is the best example of urban planning and modern architecture in India. With its wide roads, beautiful roundabouts and planned residential and commercial sectors, the City is Truly Beautiful.

Flying Down:

Direct flights to this beautiful city are from Delhi, Mumbai, Kolkata, Chennai, Hyderabad, Bengaluru, Jaipur and Ahmedabad. The highway from Delhi to Chandigarh has always been a smooth drive, but now, more so with flyovers over all intersections. By rail too, the Vande Bharat and Shatabdi trains provide easy access to the city.

Moving Around:

The first and foremost thing you should do when in Chandigarh is to drive around the city, especially the popular Sector 17 market, to get a feel of how planned the city is. Once done, head to the Sukhna Lake, the most famous attraction in Chandigarh. Frequented by morning walkers, joggers, couples on a romantic date or families on a picnic, this man-made lake is a go-to place for locals and tourists alike. You can even go boating in the lake.

The other major attraction of Chandigarh known worldwide is the Rock Garden. An open-air exhibition of sculptures made out of urban and industrial waste, designed by renowned sculptor Nek Chand. The Rock Garden is spread over a massive 40 acres, showcasing sculptures made out of terracotta, lights, broken toilet pots, bottles, etc. It is truly a sight to behold and a must-visit.

The Rose Garden of Chandigarh is also an ideal evening out. It has 825 varieties of flowers and more than 32,000 varieties of plants and trees. The various roundabouts with blooming flowers, too, are a treat. There is even a competition organised to choose the best roundabout.

Another park that you can visit is the Japanese Garden which is in two parts connected through a tunnel. The well-groomed park has pagods, Buddha statues, waterfalls and meditation areas, providing a peaceful atmosphere for the public. Another peaceful green area in the city is the Garden of Silence which boasts of a massive Buddha sculpture with lush and blooming greenery all around.

Located some 15 km from the city is the Pinjore Gardens built during the 17th century, designed in Mughal style. The terraced garden has small cascading waterfalls, fountains and water bodies, all landscaped into well-preserved greenery set amidst the backdrop of the Shivaliks. It's a perfect evening pastime for tourists.

There are a number of other gardens and fitness trails that have been built in Chandigarh which is why it is widely regarded as a peaceful, green, retirement city.

Other places to visit in the city are the National Gallery of Portraits, housing photographs of freedom fighters; the Natural History Museum; the Fateh Burj, the tallest tower in India, signifying the battle between Banda Bahadur Singh and Mughal Emperor Wazir Khan; Museum of the Evolution of Life; Le Corbusier Centre and the Open Hand monument at the Capitol Complex designed by Le Corbusier.

The most famous temple in Chandigarh is the Chandi Mandir, after which the city has been named. Situated in the cantonment area, the temple is dedicated to Chandi Mata, a form of Goddess Durga. Nearby is the Mansa Devi Temple, which is equally revered and sacred.

Stay in Comfort:

Chandigarh is flooded with hotels, literally. Some known ones are Hyatt Regency, Hyatt Centric, Radisson, The Forn Residency, Lemon Tree, Taj, The Lalit, Ramada Plaza, Wyndham, Mountview, The Oberoi, etc.

What to Buy:

Punjabi suits and Phulkari dupattas. For this, head to the famous Sector 17 market or the newly opened Elante Mall where you can buy all national and foreign brands. While shopping or moving around the city, go to the dhabas behind Sector 12 market to have tandoori Punjabi paranthas, which are to die for.

Puri

•••

On the Map:

Located on the East Coast of India, Puri has great religious significance. It is home to the revered Jagannath Temple, making it one of the dhams (holiest of holy places) in the Hindu religion that one must visit during one's lifetime. Around 60 km south of the capital of Odisha, Bhubaneswar, Puri is also renowned for the longest golden beach in India. It is home to temples, mathas, ashrams and architectural masterpieces.

Flying Down:

The nearest airport to Puri is Bhubaneswar, though there are news reports that a smaller airport at Puri is in the works. Being the state capital, Bhubaneswar is connected to all the major cities in the country, making it easy to visit Puri. The highway network too connects Puri well with South and Eastern parts of the country. The same goes for rail.

Moving Around:

When in Puri, the first stop has to be the famed Jagannath Temple built in the 11th century by King Indrayumna. Built in the Oriya style of architecture, the Temple is dedicated to Lord Jagannath aka Krishna, an avatar of Lord Vishnu. The Jagannath Temple today is one of the Char Dhams apart from the other three namely Badrinath, Dwarka and Rameshwaram.

The Temple is famous for its annual Ratha Yatra in which the three principal deities – Jagannath, Subhadra and Balabhadra – are pulled by ropes tied to their respective chariots. Unlike other temples across India, the idols of the deities in the Jagannath Temple are made of wood and not stone. The idol is changed every 12 or 19 years.

The Temple complex is a marvel. In the true Kalinga style of architecture, the gates, walls, pillars, etc, are all covered with intricate designs and sculptures. The main temple is perched atop an elevated stone platform and the whole complex is surrounded by two walls, with the outer one known as Meghanada Pracira and the inner one known as Kurma Pracira.

Near the Jagannath Temple is the Narendra Tank, a holy water body believed to have been built in the 15th century. An island in the middle of the lake is home to a small temple called Chandana Mandapa.

Some other temples you can visit are the Sakshi Gopal Temple, Lakshmi Temple, Vimala Temple, Gundicha Temple, Alarnatha Temple and Mausima Temple.

Apart from the Jagannatha Temple, the other major attraction of Puri is its beaches, with the Puri Beach in the city supposed to have the softest sand in the world. Other beaches around Puri are the Swargdwar Beach, Baliharachandi Beach and the Balighai Beach. However, it is the first two beaches – Puri Beach and the Swargdwar Beach – that most tourists flock to, being in the centre of the city along its marine drive. In the evenings, the beaches are full of tourists and locals, with stalls of eateries and hawkers all around.

When on a visit to Puri, it is advisable to keep an extra day to see the unique Sun Temple at Konark. Around 35 km from Puri, the 13th-century temple is an architectural marvel and a designated UNESCO World Heritage Site. Dedicated to the Sun God, the Konark Temple is built in the form of a giant chariot drawn by seven horses. The remains of the magnificent temple show the intricate designs and its meticulously planned architecture.

The Sun Temple in the olden days was a landmark for sailors to locate the shore. The wheels of the chariot so engraved, also double up as ancient clocks, with each wheel having eight spokes. Each spoke represents a prahar (three hours) and hence eight spokes represent 24 hours.

So much for an ancient clock!

Stay in Comfort:

Being a beach city, Puri is full of beach resorts or beach facing properties like Toshali Sands, Hotel Lucky India, Hotel Golden Palace, The Hans Coco Palms, Pride Ananya Resort and The Chariot Resort and Spa. There are several dharamshalas, ashrams and guest houses too in the city, owned by various religious organisations.

What to Buy:

Puja and devotional items, idols of Lord Jagannath, pattachitra paintings, wooden replicas of the chariot and Oriya sarees like Sambalpuri, Bomkai, Bapta and Sonepuri. Visit the famous artists village, Raghurajpur, on the Bhubaneswar highway to buy arts and crafts from local people. Each home has a wide variety of art displayed in their rooms and aangans. Must visit for those who want to buy a piece of Odisha.

Ranchi

•●•

On the Map:

The Capital of Jharkhand, Ranchi is located in the southern part of the Chhota Nagpur Plateau that forms the eastern end of the Deccan Plateau. Also known as the City of Waterfalls, Ranchi is surrounded by flat-topped hills and lush greenery and boasts a vibrant tribal culture with deep historical roots.

Flying Down:

Being the capital of a state, Ranchi is well connected to all the major cities in India through direct flights to Delhi, Mumbai, Kolkata, Chennai, Hyderabad and Bengaluru. The Vande Bharat connects it with Varanasi, while all major high-speed trains going towards West Bengal and North-East go via Ranchi. The road network has improved in the past 10 years and today the city is well-connected with Varanasi, Patna and Kolkata.

Moving Around:

The first place to visit in Ranchi is the Ranchi lake. Constructed in 1842, the lake is at the base of Ranchi Hill, atop is a Shiva Temple that gives panoramic views of the city and the valley beyond.

Another temple that is located on a hilltop is the Jagannath Temple. The Temple is a replica of the main Puri Temple and is replete with carvings, sculptures and intricate designs. Other temples in the city worth a visit are the Pahari Mandir, Angrabadi Temple Complex and the Sun Temple.

The Rock Garden along the Kanke Dam, is a perfect evening or weekend out for locals. It is replete with waterfalls, sculptures, art and a view of unparalleled beauty. The Ram Dayal Munda Park, named after the renowned scholar, is a favourite among joggers and evening walkers. The Biodiversity Park is another lush green spot in the city popular among city dwellers.

Ranchi is known for its many waterfalls located in and around the city. Some of the more accessible ones are Dassam Falls, located some 26 km from the city; the Joshna Falls 31 km from Ranchi, cascading from a height of 45 metres and surrounded by lush greenery; the Panch Gagh Falls, probably nearest to the city has five falls cascading down through steep hills; the Sita Falls located 34 km from Ranchi that look a miniature Niagara and the Hudru Falls that will take your breath away as they fall from a height of 320 feet.

Apart from waterfalls, one drive you must take is to Patratu, a small town in Ramgarh district, some 40 km from Ranchi. The road that goes downhill from Ranchi into the Patratu Valley is simply mesmerising. It twists and turns through lush green wooded forest, winding its way down into an area that is surrounded by hills, water bodies and green surroundings.

The highlight, of course, is the Patratu Dam, where you can sit along its shore and look at the waters beyond, forgetting your worries in its shimmer!

Stay in Comfort:

I have been travelling to Ranchi for the last 10 years and whenever I used to go, the best hotels used to be Capitol Hill and Chanakya BNR Hotel. But now international brands too, have set up shop there, namely Radisson Blu and Le Lac Sarovar Portico. Apart from these, the other options are in the three and two-star categories.

What to Buy:

You can easily buy Dokra art figurines and sculptures from the state government emporium, Jharcraft. Apart from that, you can also go in for bamboo and wood products, tussar sarees from Godda, metal artefacts and tribal jewellery.

Nashik and Shirdi

• • •

On the Map:

Located on the banks of the Godavari River, Nashik is one of the fastest growing cities in India today. The city is also known as the Wine Capital of India, being home to many vineyards and wineries. It is also a religious centre as Kumbh Mela is organised here once every 12 years. Nashik is also home to the Triyambakeshwar Jyotirlinga and Shirdi – the home of the revered spiritual leader, Sai Baba – around 95 km away.

Flying Down:

While flights to Nashik from Delhi and Hyderabad have commenced recently, Shirdi is well connected to various metros via direct flights from Delhi, Hyderabad, Bengaluru, Chennai and Indore. The newly launched Hindu Hrudaysamrat Balasaheb Thackeray Maharashtra Samrudhi Mahamarg passes via Shirdi and near Nashik, making connectivity by road easy and comfortable. The rail network too is well entrenched here.

Moving Around:

The first stop at Shirdi has to be the Shri Sai Baba Sansthan Temple, the lifeline of the town's economy. One of the most revered shrines in India, the Temple can be visited for normal darshan as well as for aarti which takes place at different times of the day. Bookings can be made through the Sai Baba Shirdi App.

Other places associated with the Sai Baba are located near the main temple. You can visit Dwarkamai first, the place where the Saint used to spend most of his time, including his last days. Next to Dwarkamai is Chavadi, where the great Sai Baba used to spend alternate nights. Opposite the Chavadi is the Abdul Baba cottage, the place where the closest devotee of Sai Baba used to live. You can also visit the Khandoba Mandir, a temple dedicated to the presiding deity of Shirdi.

An extremely interesting place to visit in Shirdi is the Sai Teerth, a devotional theme park that has attractions for all age groups. You can start by boarding a train that moves on a track showcasing the biggest and most sacred temples of India. The bogey stops at each life-size replica of the temple for a few seconds to enable you to savour the visual spectacle. The theme park also runs shows like the

Lanka Dahan 5D show; "Sabka Malik Ek", a show on the teachings of the Sai Baba.

On the outskirts of Shirdi is the Sai Heritage Village which showcases major events in the life of the Sai Baba through life-size sculptures.

65 km from Shirdi is the revered Shani Shingnapur, a village where there are no doors and locks. The village revolves around the Shani Dev Temple, with the temple itself being exquisitely built with deepalayas in the shape of stupas and an underground route that connects the temple complex with the parking and shopping area.

Moving on to Nashik, which is one of the most sacred cities in the country. It is also here that the Kumbh Mela takes place once every 12 years on the banks of the River Godavari. Panchvati, the place where Lord Rama, Goddess Sita and Lord Lakshman stayed while in exile, is frequented by hundreds of pilgrims on a daily basis. Panchvati means Garden of Five Banyan Trees and you can still see the trees there. The trees are believed to have existed since the days of the Ramayana. You can also visit the Sita Gufa nearby and the Kalaram Temple, which has statues of the deities in black.

Near Nashik are two Hindu pilgrimage sites – the Saptashrungi Temple and Trimbakeshwar Jyotirlinga. The Saptashrungi Temple is surrounded by seven mountain peaks and is considered as a half Shaktipeeth, of the three-and-a-half Shaktipeeth's in Maharashtra. The temple is approachable via more than 500 steps or a ropeway, which takes two minutes.

One of the 12 Jyotirlingas in the country, Trimbakeshwar is located at the foothills of the Brahmagiri Hills and is also located close to a Kund which is the source of the Godavari River.

Another historical place that one must visit when in Nashik is the Pandu Leni or the Trirashmi Caves. The carvings here date back to 3rd Century BC and 2nd Century AD and depict the Hinayana Buddhism beliefs.

Around Nashik are a number of waterfalls like the Dugarwadi waterfalls, Dudhsagar and Vihigaon. Surrounded by hills and rocks, the area also boasts of famous treks like the one to the Dhodap, Salher, Ahivantgad, Mulher and the Anjaneri Fort.

Nashik is also home to the famous Sula Vineyards, which has a resort and organises wine growing and tasting sessions for tourists.

Stay in Comfort:

Shirdi is flooded with hotels and dhabas. They seem to be more in number than houses. Some good options are Hotel Temple Tree, Hotel Sun n' Sand, Renest Shradha Inn and Starlit Suites.

Nashik, on the other hand, has few branded properties like The Gateway Hotel Ambad, Holiday Inn Express, Courtyard by Marriott, Radisson Blu and Regenta Resort Soma Vine Village.

What to Buy:

Shirdi is a shopper's paradise. You get everything ranging from puja items, sculptures of Sai Baba, bangles, home furnishings, sarees and suit material in Paithani style. Nashik too is famous for textiles, art and handicrafts.

Shivamogga

• • •

On the Map:

A non-descript city in Central Karnataka is suddenly seeing an influx of business travellers and tourists after the opening of a swanky airport. Located on the foothills of the Western Ghats, the city is surrounded by lush green forests that are home to various wild animals and a big source of attraction for tourists. The district also boasts of many historical and cultural centres that are a major draw too.

Flying Down:

Shivamogga is now connected by air to Bengaluru, Hyderabad and Goa. The airport has recently opened and connectivity to other cities is expected to improve in the future. By road, it is a nearly 6 hour drive from Bengaluru and being in the centre of Karnataka, all major trains make a stop here.

Moving Around:

While the city itself does not have much to see, it is the surrounding area that will captivate you. 12 km away is the Gajanur Dam, a reservoir on the Tunga River that spreads across acres. The Dam is the main source of drinking water for many wild animals living in the forest encircling it.

Next to the Dam is the Sakrebayalu Elephant Camp, where one can see elephants being trained. Early morning everyday, the elephants walk down to the reservoir to take bath and play in the water, drawing tourists in large numbers.

To see the big cats, some 9 km away, is the Tyavarekoppa Wildlife Sanctuary, where amidst the flora and fauna, you can also see the elusive animal in all its glory.

Further down the Tunga reservoir, deep inside the forest, you will come onto Agumbe, a famous sunset point that gives you a glimpse of the rich bio-diversity of the area. Agumbe is also famous for being the place where the famous TV series Malgudi Days was shot.

The Bhadra Dam on the River Bhadra is an attraction that is not to be missed for its flora and fauna. The area is also home to many waterfalls like the Dabbe Falls, Achakanya Falls, Unchalli Falls, Barkana and Onake Abbi Falls and the most famous Jog Falls. Jog Falls are usually referred to as the Niagara Falls of India. The Jog Falls are nearly 100 km from Shimoga and are a part of the Sharavathi River. They are the second highest plunge after the Nohkalikai Falls in Meghalaya and reach their splendour during the monsoon.

You can also trek to a few peaks to witness nature's full glory. There is the Kodachari Peak, some 115 km from Shivamogga and the Kundadri, a single-formation rock which is very popular with trekkers.

Shivamogga is also home to two villages where everyone speaks in Sanskrit. The twin villages of Hosahalli and Mattur perfectly blend the ancient with the modern.

Situated on the banks of the Krishna River is an ancient Shiva Temple named Kedareshwara Temple. Built in the 11th century, the Temple also has a unique Swarg Mandap to perform puja rituals. Near the city is also the Rameshwara Temple in Keladi which in the past has served as the Capital of the Keladi Nayaka Kingdom.

Engulfed in greenery are the ruins of the Kavaledurga Fort. The ancient hill fort is located inside a forest and makes for a great trek through lush greenery.

Stay in Comfort:

Shivamogga does not have many comfort hotels. There are only two branded properties – The Fern and Royal Orchid, with the latter being located in the city centre. Both offer luxurious rooms and great food.

What to Buy:

Apart from silk sarees, you can buy local handicrafts, rosewood carvings, sandalwood and wooden toys from Shivamogga. Markets are full of clothing and jewellery, much to a shopper's delight.

The spectacular view from the State Beach Resort in Kannur

The Mahalaxmi Temple in Kolhapur

The awe-inspiring architecture of the Chamundeswari Temple in Mysuru

The breathtaking Adiyogi Shiva Bust outside Coimbatore

The exquisite Mehrangarh Fort in Jodhpur

The picturesque Lake Palace in Udaipur

The Jatayu sculpture outside Kollam in Kerala

The Kailasa Temple in Ellora carved out of a single rock

The Krishna-Godavari Sangam outside Vijaywada

The breathtakingly beautiful Brihadesvara Temple in Thanjavur

Photographs Sources:

Varun Soni; Wikipedia; Wikimedia; Trawell.in; Tricitytoday.com; thesouthfirst.com; hotelierindia.com; abhibus; prembhakti.in; kesari.in; housing.com; mylovieus.com; medium.com; thomascook.in; WordPress.com and Tripadvisor.com

Printed in the USA
CPSIA information can be obtained
at www.ICGtesting.com
CBHW020811301124
18176CB00047BA/720